"A  *part Thru the Looking Glass... funny and moving and real... A Tocqueville-ian journey for actors plying their craft in a new, international era."*

Robert Hupp, Artistic Director, The Rep, Little Rock.

www.therep.org

An Actor Walks into China is a wonderfully idiosyncratic view into the mysterious world of The Middle Kingdom and the yet more mysterious world of the inside of an actor's head. If you've ever thought of going to China or shared, as I have, a dressing room with Colin McPhillamy then this book will explain a lot that you should know.

Christopher Campbell, Literary Manager, Royal Court Theatre.

"A colorful, perceptive, highly amusing and beautifully descriptive view of a Western actor gently maneuvering his way through the minefield of an alien lifestyle... great comedic story-telling...a book where you can see, smell, touch, feel and enjoy the writer's exploration and acceptance of an unfamiliar and intriguing way of life. The linguistic misunderstandings, the red tape, the difficulties and occasional discomfort are gently put to one side as the author comes to know and respect the country and its people. "AN ACTOR WALKS INTO CHINA" is not to be missed.

Joan Lane, Producer, Wild Thyme Productions.
http://www.wildthymeproductions.com

"...the extremely funny tale of an actor's perilous journey into cross-cultural theatrical production with the world's fastest-growing nation. McPhillamy initially seduces us with his love for China, its voraciously intelligent and sheltered students and their thirst to understand Shakespeare. It is both deeply moving and irresistibly charming. Later, he ambitiously embarks on a co-production between China and the UK that quickly descends into something akin to juggling chainsaws whilst cycling on quicksand..."

JB Blanc, actor. www.Jbblanc.com

"A witty, wise, warm and wonderful read. Colin McPhillamy is a unique talent with a voice like none other. His view of life, with all its remarkable, funny and unexpected messiness, is both hilarious and touching."

Andy Jordan, Director and Producer, Andy Jordan Productions.

http://www.andyjordanproductions.co.uk

'A charming, funny & sensitive look at cultural differences, Chinese social quirks and the war between art and commerce that goes on in any land by a charming, funny & sensitive actor.'

ROY SMILES, playwright, author of YING TONG, PYTHONESQUE and KURT & SID.

"Wonderfully entertaining, full of humor and insight, with a delicious turn of phrase that evoked an almost visceral sense of place and atmosphere. A fresh, sparkling take on life in modern China."

Dr. Jennifer Kloester www.jenniferkloester.com

"This is a journey to China by a multi-talented actor/writer/director/teacher/producer, and it holds lessons and insights that go beyond any border. McPhillamy does have a way with words, and while his writing and acting credits attest to that, his humor and timing especially shine through in this collection. There is much to ponder, and much to enjoy in this quick read. Can anyone say, Encore?"

Mary "Casey" Martin, columnist for HOOPLA and FJORDS REVIEW

http://homebrewpress.com

"I couldn't help thinking, as I read this book, that the UN would do well to co-opt Colin McPhillamy as advisor in dialogues between China and "the West." A work filled with grace and gentle joy, not to mention the wisdom of insight, borne of excruciatingly painful observation, achingly patient listening and abundantly generous humor."

David Conolly, Melbourne, Australia.

"Mandatory reading for anyone thinking of setting up a business deal in China...

full of affection, insight, humor, and with such a light touch re the politics..."

Barrie Hesketh, Cheshire, UK.

http://williamshakespearedarkphoenix.blogspot.com

For anyone who loves theatre and traveling, "An Actor Walks into China" is one to read. The anecdotes of his experiences in acting in China with his irrepressible friend Joe Graves are not only informative of the craft and culture, but also entertaining and very moving. Don't miss this great book."

Justin Adams, playwright, actor (The Miracle Worker) Beijing, www.justincadams.com

"A delightful and worthwhile book, full of kindness, wisdom and humor."

Janine Arundel, Sydney, Australia.

"...delightful and immersive and it makes me crazy nostalgic for a return trip (toxic smog and chicken dishes consisting mostly of beak be damned). It is a beautiful and unusual memoir about a beautiful and unusual place and its people."

Jason O' Connell, actor (Edgar) King Lear, Beijing.

An Actor Walks into China

colin McPhillamy

Also by Colin McPhillamy
The Tree House and Other Stories

© Copyright Colin McPhillamy 2013
All rights reserved.

ISBN: 148111297X
ISBN-13: 9781481112970

Dedication

To Joe Graves,
a truly amazing man of theater—
an inspiration.

Or as I sometimes think of him,
the man whose fault it all was.

Colin McMillan

Disclaimer

I went to Beijing in 2008, again in 2009 and 2012. I was the London producer on a week-long festival of Chinese theater in London in 2012. Those are facts. The account that follows is highly fictionalized. I have changed almost all of the names of people, places and events, hoping to discover humor in my telling of some of the cultural confusions which arose. Furthermore, certain details throughout have been altered for purposes of storytelling. These changes are intended as a courtesy.

But some of it happened, and quite a bit of it is true. Or is that the other way around?

Acknowledgements

This slim volume was written on the road. I would like to thank everybody who gave me hospitality while I was traveling. Valerie Tarrant, Michael Shaw, Peter Johnston, David Conolly, Cecilia and Mark Currey, Alan Conolly and Elizabeth Ramsay, JB Blanc, Janine and Humphrey Arundel, Francine Bates and Russell Campbell, Terry Kilburn, Nicola Nimmo, Tamara Brooks and Theo Bikell, Peter Thompson and Jan Puffer, Emily Bly and Jonathan Pytell.

Thanks to Philip Aldridge, Mark Carey, and Barrie Hesketh, who read early drafts, and made invaluable suggestions. I am indebted to Patricia Conolly who listened patiently to more than one telling of the story, and for splendid editorial input! Thanks to everyone who hosted the performance versions, and to all those who attended and offered encouragement. To Nan Barnet and Gordon McConnell in Lake Worth, Barbara Dirickson in Los Angeles, Dr. Jon Hallberg of the Mill City Clinic, Minneapolis and Sheila

Livingston of The Guthrie Theater who made that introduction, Susan and Jim Lenfesty in Minneapolis, David Bruson in New York, Kathy Towson and Haley Channing for assistance, Michael Kingsbury of the White Bear Theatre, London, Mark Carey for arranging the Village Hall in Illmington, and Janine Arundel for arranging the Community Centre in North Sydney.

Thanks to Joan Lane and to Fred Walker for invaluable production consultancy. General thanks to all those professionals who worked so hard to achieve smooth operations in various international contexts. For reasons of discretion I will not be more specific than that, but they know who they are and I thank them.

Thanks to Robert Hupp at The Rep in Little Rock, not only for his fine production of the Sherlock Holmes play where I played Dr. Watson, but for reasons beyond that. It is fair to say that without him, this book could not have been written.

Thanks to Miss Lang and to Miss Xu, for help with pinyin Chinese, any errors that remain in the text are, of course, my own.

As this book is self-published, I thank the friendly folk at CreateSpace who offer excellent book design, editing, and formatting services.

Finally, I also make an acknowledgement to the civic and political freedoms that I count myself fortunate to have grown up with, and now enjoy as a citizen. It is nice to live in a jurisdiction where the publication of such a book will not—one hopes—lead to confinement in a small space with poor diet.

Contents

Preface	xv
An Actor Walks Into China	1
The Middle Kingdom Looms	31
Man of La Mancha	39
Air Miles	57
Political!?	99
Why?	107

Preface

I started out to write an account of my experiences in China. While I worked, a tangle of smaller stories which also wanted to be told, broke cover. I wrote these other stories and then I found they had no place in this book. A couple of insights made the work worth doing, though. For example, I realized that I would never have gone to the Middle Kingdom if I hadn't come to America.

Put another way, I thought the story would be about a certain thing, and it turned out to be about something else, and then not about that. That would correspond neatly to adventures in a realm where not everything is as it seems. Somewhere, perhaps, like China.

I liked everyone I met in China. In personal interactions, I met with warmth, hospitality, and friendship.

One time I was on a crowded bus in Beijing. To my considerable embarrassment, an elderly lady, seeing I was the lone stranger on board, vacated her seat and pushed, pulled and generally manhandled me until I was sitting in it. My protestations were useless. She was an unstoppable force. We communicated with smiles and laughter, and most people on the bus thought it was funny too.

In the brief time I taught English at Beijing University, I was incredibly impressed by the institution and the students. I was treated with exemplary respect and courtesy, and their diligence was astonishing. One young lady exchanged language practice with me once a week at lunch.

"Can we discuss politics?" I asked tentatively.

"Of course," she said.

"What about the revolution?" I asked.

"Which one?" she countered. "We have so many."

In dealings with Chinese theatrical professionals I met people who were dynamic and passionate, and I felt that we shared a delight in what might be achieved. I came away from my experiences in China full of admiration for the people, and for the transformational achievements of the past few decades.

It was only in the nitty-gritty of a business environment that the shouting started.

My life as an actor has pitched itself somewhere between a holiday and a party, and in my line they pay you in fun. My work has taken me from the Orkney Islands off the northern tip of Scotland to South Australia and many places in between. I've toured in Europe and the Middle East, I've worked in the West End, at the Royal National Theatre in London, at theaters off-West

End and off-off-Broadway, on Broadway too, at many places in the United States, at festivals in Australia, and at the Sydney Theatre Company. I feel like I get around.

None of the above prepared me for China.

An Actor Walks Into China

An Actor Walks Into China

The first time I applied for a visa at the Chinese consulate on Forty-second Street and Twelfth Avenue in New York City, the lady behind the glass asked me my occupation.

"Writer." I told her.

"Writer! What kind of writer? Political!?"

As a British citizen living in America, not at that time an American citizen, it crossed my mind to quip, "Political? I don't even vote." But in the time it took to think it, I realized this would be a fine example of cross-cultural humor not traveling well.

Put another way, *Ni zai Nio Yue jiang yi ge xiao hua, dan shi Bei Jing de ren bu jue de hao xiao. Wei shen me ne? Yin wei ta men ting bu dao.*

Which means, "You can tell a joke in New York, and they won't laugh in Beijing. Why not? Well, they can't hear it."

And let's remember that, in China, voting is not widely practiced.

Of course, consular matters can get a little odd, even surreal, in any direction. Consider the case of my friend Zhang Yue, who applied for an American green card. The final interview occurred in one of the Southern states.

The official said, "It says here that you are a communist."

"Yes, that's right."

"I don't understand how anybody could be a communist."

"In my country, it's a great honor. I joined the Party when I was eight years old."

"But I just don't understand how anybody could be a communist."

This went on for about half an hour. Finally Yue said, "Look! It's like Catholicism. Nobody really believes it, but everybody says they do!"

"Oh, I get it!" The official stamped the form. Yue got the green card.

My Chinese adventure began in Philadelphia, in the United States of America. If this were a film, the pre-credits opening sequence would find me retailing my commodity—my British accent. I was playing a real-life man named Wallace Greenslade, known to millions in the 1950s as the voice of the BBC. This was in a play called *Ying Tong* about the pre-Monty Python funny guys, the Goons, pioneers of the surreal in modern comedy.

My New York agent, Sam Silver, called me one morning with the news that they were doing a Sherlock Holmes play in Little Rock, Arkansas. I was interested. In fact, I was more interested than Sam was—a detail I mention here because some years later, he and I had a singular breakfast together, but I'll tell you about it when we get there.

Meanwhile, the sometime leader of the free world was one of Arkansas's most famous sons and the retail outlet for Chinese manufacturing known as Wal-Mart took its rise there. I felt a compulsion to get down to the Natural State, as they call it, immediately, and try to find out what was in the water there.

So there I was a little while later, playing Dr. Watson in Little Rock. One night, waiting to go onstage, I turned to the man playing Sherlock Holmes and said, "Joe, do you know what you are doing next?"

He said, "Yes, I'm directing and I'm playing King Lear. In Beijing."

And I said, "Who's playing Kent?"

And he said, "Why don't you play Kent?"

And that was what a screenplay theorist would call, The Inciting Incident.

China, huh? All I knew about China, when I was a kid in London in the 1960s, was that no one I knew ever went there. In those days China was closed, hidden, a mystery. With that in mind, since I became an actor I've often felt that I was walking into China. Certainly, when I came to America from Britain it might as well have been China, except that it wasn't—the real China came later.

I admit to becoming fascinated by the place, and Joe Graves, the man who took me there, told me to be careful, because that's what happened to him, and now look.

In 1983 the late great American playwright Arthur Miller, was invited to direct his play, Death of a Salesman, in Beijing. He wrote a book about the experience. Such an invitation could not have happened a decade earlier. It was significant and successful in that it opened the way for other such invitations, and for cultural exchanges to occur. That process took a little time, but now exchanges are frequent.

Joe Graves was also invited to direct a play at that same theater about a decade and a half later. Joe directed a production of Thornton Wilder's, *Our Town*. He used some student actors from Peking University. One of the eminent scholars from that distinguished institution said something to the effect, "I've studied Western classical literature for a long time, but I do not know how to put on a play. Could you show us?"

It was a gracious invitation.

The following year Joe made arrangements to return to Beijing. He was given hospitality by the university and he posted a notice that he would be holding auditions for a production of Shakespeare's *The Tempest*. Joe would direct, and also play Prospero. There was huge interest from the students. Several thousand wanted to be involved. By working ten hours a day for six days, Joe managed to see four hundred of them and to cast fifty in the play. There was very little money for the production budget. He thought that rope would be a good option to use as backdrop and set. Rope is flexible, adaptable, has maritime associations and above all, it's cheap.

However, as every stage manager knows, you never pay retail. Rope was retailing at 600 yuan ($75 approx. at 2000 prices) per hundred meters in central Beijing, but Joe found a supplier in a village two miles beyond the capital, who could do it for one tenth that rate. He and one of the students took at taxi (the subway was a lot less developed back then) to the end of the road—literally. They made the rest of the journey on a mule. Through the snow. The show was a popular event and was the presager of the now well-established PKU Institute of World Theatre and Film of which Joe is the Artistic Director.

Word of the show spread to all sorts of places throughout China, including somewhere far west of Xian. From that distant locale an invitation was issued and Joe managed to broker funding to take the cast of The Tempest on tour. When they reached the outdoor amphitheater where they were to play, they were told that a regional music festival was playing that night.

"It's either your play or the music festival." Said the local director.

"Let's do both." Said Joe.

So they did. They'd play a scene and then some musicians would play a set. Sometimes they'd play alongside the actors, underscoring the action. Sometimes a soloist would come and play while the actors gave focus. Long after midnight the performance came to a close.

There was no applause.

Instead, the cast and all the musicians stood at the edge of the stage while the audience, three thousand of them, filed past and touched their knees silently as an expression of appreciation.

Listening to these tales, I realized that when I thought Little Rock, Arkansas was as exotic as my theatrical travels were going to get—I was wrong.

I arrived in Beijing a month after the 2008 Olympics.

The famous Beijing air had been given a respite during the Games because the burning of domestic trash had been put on hold, and they had cut the traffic in half by requiring people to drive only on alternate days. But now they were clearing the trash backlog, and the traffic was back in full force. This meant that most nights the air became a thick yellow-greenish-brownish toxic mist, and visibility was reduced to ten paces. I had experienced this once before as a small child in London. I walked through the very last pea-soup fog—given that name by Charles Dickens. The air was so thick, I could not see my uncle's face, so I gripped his hand tightly. Getting rid of the pea-soupers was simple. Londoners stopped burning toxic waste in their homes and the air got better.

We were housed in a tower block on the fourteenth floor. At ground level there was a small plaza where local people would do Tai Chi exercises in the mornings. The internal corridors of the block would light up if you stomped your feet, otherwise they were dark. That first night I lay awake, excited at the exotic sensation of just being in this mysterious country. Far below in the street, two cats were auditioning for the Peking Opera.

Beijing is a modern city—at least it is now, but it wasn't fifteen years ago. That first time I was there, from my apartment window in Lin Da Bei Lu, I watched a tower block being constructed at the speed at which, overnight, bamboo springs six feet into the air. The construction workers were bivouacked in large tents that slept ten or twelve, which were pitched on the concrete pavements. It was October, and the cold of the winter was coming.

I went to the usual places a visitor would go: the Forbidden City, Tiananmen Square, the Summer Palace and the Great Wall. Not far from the Great Hall of the People there is a little piece of the old city left. I wandered up and down a few crowded lanes looking for a hutong. One afternoon I took a ride on the number-thirteen subway line, which is a loop through the northern Beijing suburbs. I was the only Westerner on the train and people stared at me.

That year the government decreed that everyone in Beijing would learn one hundred phrases of English to prepare for the games. As I looked from one of the number-thirteen subway cars into the forests of new tower blocks, appearing through the gloomy air like an M. C. Escher drawing, I saw English on the bilingual street signs. Once decided, policy gets implemented in

China, whether it works or not. "We are arriving at Wudaokou...at Shangdi...at Xi Er Qi." said a Chinese lady in English through the public address system as the train pulled into each station.

The subway system in Beijing began in the early 1960s with consultation from the Soviet Union. It took a long time to build, and for several decades there was just one line running east and west through the city. When China opened up, the system got a little impetus and a few more lines were added. The 2008 Olympic Games were the real spur. Now there is a spaghetti of subway lines all over the city, with complex plans for more.

And then there are the roads. The city is built around five concentric-ring roads of the urban freeway type. The capital of China is three times the size of Los Angeles. Twenty million people live there, about as many as in the entire continent of Australia.

Picture a highway, four lanes in each direction, separated by a median strip lined with young trees, then a further median strip at the edges of the highway, and two more lanes with more young trees, making twelve lanes in all—six in each direction. And this twelve-lane highway crossed, at right angles, by another similar twelve-lane highway. Now fill all twenty-four lanes with buses, cars, horse-drawn carts, taxis, and bicycles—lots of bicycles, up to and including mopeds, motorbikes and tandems. Now honk the horns and turn up the volume. Add in traffic lights, and very efficient they are too though no one seems too bothered. Shove in about ten thousand pedestrians, and you have an average crossroads anywhere in the many, many square miles that is Beijing. One time I crossed one of these intersections on foot with my friend Joe Graves.

"Assume nothing," said Graves as we stepped into the traffic. "You are laboring under the occidental delusion," he yelled, when we were about halfway across and I had narrowly missed taking a bicycle in the rear, "that signs mean anything!"

We rehearsed *King Lear* in the Democracy Building—presumably so named by the Ministry of Irony—in the northwestern quadrant of the Beijing University campus. Beijing University, like many things in China, goes by several names. It retains Peking University or PKU, but it is generally called Beida, short for *Bei Jing Da Xue*. We were a mixed cast of professionals and students, Western and Chinese.

The Democracy Building exemplifies some of the finest traditional architecture in the entire city, and uniquely among the several buildings in that part of the campus, it had resident caretakers, an elderly couple who looked as though they had lived through every revolution since 1910. Every evening we rehearsed in the large hall on the second floor—a room big enough to accommodate some two hundred people. Sometimes our request for the space did not get communicated through the necessary series of offices to the elderly woman who was the Lady Keeper of the Door. On these evenings the

King Lear company would gather outside the Democracy Building and Joe would arrive, and the old woman would crack the door and unleash a stream of furious Chinese which one of the students would translate. Joe would smilingly point out that we had been here yesterday and hoped to be again tomorrow.

"Bu Shi!" the woman would say, which means, "No!"

Of course, we understood that this large building with its three floors, several offices and large hall was also this lady's home, and that maybe on some days the phone didn't ring from whatever office to say that twenty-five actors would arrive in the evening and stay late practicing their play. On those days perhaps, it was a welcome break for the lady from opening and closing the door all day and dealing with people.

But we still needed a place to rehearse, so Joe would persist and smilingly say, "Please, may we come in?"

And the Lady Keeper of the Door would say—in furious Chinese—"No one told me!" And she would slam the door in a way that said the Chairman himself wouldn't be getting inside if she hadn't been officially informed.

Joe and I talked the matter over, and we concluded that this behavior was understandable. The lady had probably endured some truly harrowing episodes during the decades of China's great challenges following the founding of the People's Republic in 1950, and now suddenly here were all these *waiguoren*—foreigners—doing all these strange activities with young Chinese kids.

We decided to offer a token of friendship. Joe purchased a large bunch of yellow roses, thinking that these were precisely the flowers that represent friendship in China. He made a solo visit to the Democracy Building where he knocked respectfully at the front door. The encounter went like this:

Joe said (in English), "I've brought you these flowers as a token of respect, friendship, and harmony."

The lady took the flowers, and holding them at arm's length while maintaining eye contact, took several backward paces until she came to a large trashcan. She dumped the roses in one swift martial motion, came back to the door, and unleashed the inevitable stream of irate Chinese. Joe says he can't be certain what she said, but he thinks it was the equivalent of the English, "I've got two words for you, and they are not 'Let's Dance!'"

That I would ever understand the stream of irate Chinese seemed unlikely, but soon after arriving I learned some of the basics of Mandarin. In general, the Chinese people I encountered to whom I tried to say something in Chinese did not appear overly impressed by what I had to offer. This is partly because it is one of the great achievements of the Chinese people that they can speak their own language, and partly because they have an unlimited supply of people already speaking it fluently, and they just don't need any more. And partly because it is so damn difficult for a Westerner to learn. But I persisted, and after a while I could fluently say, *"Ni hao, wo bu hui shuo putonghua,*" which means, "Hi, I don't speak Mandarin"...I think. Of course, if you get the tones wrong it could mean, "Why is your nose so huge?" You don't believe me? Try this:

"Wo xiang yao yi ge pingguo": "I would like an apple."

"Wo xiang yao ni de pigu": "I would like your backside."

This is how wars get started.

But the effort to learn even entry-level phrases in Chinese was not wasted. One night I was running late and wondering if the front door of the Democracy Building would be closed. The Lady Keeper of the Door only deigned to open it once during the evening. How would I get inside and join the rehearsal?

By chance the door was still open. I sprinted for it, and I arrived marginally ahead of the Lady Keeper of the Door, who also put on a burst of speed from within. I used my right foot as a doorstop.

Taking a chance with the tones I plunged straight ahead. *"Wanshang hao,"* I said, *"Jintian nin hao ma?":* "Good evening, how are you (using the polite form of 'you') today?"

Centuries of etiquette demanded a response. *"Wo hao, ni ne?"* she said: "I'm fine, and you?"

"Wo ye hen hao, xie xie, xie xie nin wen le wo." : "I'm just peachy too, thank you. Thanks for asking."

The old lady regarded me with suspicion. Slowly she released the door. My foot was mildly bruised, but I got in.

Our production was double cast. Lear's daughters were played by three Chinese girls and also by three American girls. In rehearsal they would alternate, sometimes mixing and matching because not everyone was always available. The Americans worked as descendants of the best of Western acting, looking for that famous, most elusive quality, "truth". They would try to feel things authentically, and would ask questions of the characters they were playing, such as, "What is she going through right now?" The Asian girls were poised and still. They asked no such questions. They spoke clearly. They were graceful.

We rehearsed at night. In the mornings I taught an English conversation class. But the jet lag—there being exactly twelve hours between Beijing and New York—got me up early. So before the class I would take breakfast, which was fun. From about 6:00 a.m. mobile carts with hot plates abound in the Beijing streets. A *jian bing* is a pancake with spring onions and spices, you could add *yi ge jidan* (an egg) or some *zhu rou* (bacon) and some *mian bao* (a muffin), and that costs three and a half kuai—about half a dollar. Outside in the bracing Beijing air, you can't call it "fresh" this famous air, the family with whom I struck up an acquaintance would laugh at my stumbling attempts to talk to them, and they would talk back to me as though to a deaf person when trying to get an answer. *"Ni xiang yao la ma!?"* At first I thought they were saying something along the lines of "I'll rip your vocal cords out." But actually they were only enquiring whether I wanted the spicy relish.

You could get a similar combination of carbs, protein and seasonings, although with a higher sugar content, at one of the many available McDonald's, where you would pay the Western price—eighteen kuai, about three dollars at today's prices. In the corporate processed environment hinting at middle-management initiatives, the service sometimes came with the retail resentment that one encounters in the West.

The students at Beida are uncommonly bright. Peking University is called the Harvard of the East. Competition for a spot is fierce. The number of yearly applicants runs in the millions, and the intake is about twenty-five thousand.

In one class I told an old joke, "How do you get to Carnegie Hall? You gotta practice!"

The boy on my left mumbled, "I am too shy."

Later on I learned something about this boy's background. The fee for annual tuition at Beida is around 5,000 RMB a year—at today's prices, that's about $830 a year. Negligible, right? Right. Unless you happen to be a farmer in Southern China for whom the price of a cup of coffee in sophisticated Beijing would represent a week's wages. The shy boy was undoubtedly the smartest person he had ever known. He was the smartest in his village, in his school, maybe in his whole province. When the letter of acceptance from Beida arrived, his mother and father and everyone in the village sat down to figure out how they were going to come up with the money to pay the tuition. Then the shy boy got to Beida, and suddenly everyone was as smart as he is. He and many children like him operate under huge pressure during their college years.

But I didn't know any of this that morning in class, so I said, in tonally inaccurate Mandarin, *"Ru guo ni xiang shuo Ying wen, na me ni bi xu mei tian lian xi."* : "If you want to speak English you must practice every day." The kids laughed at my syntax and pronunciation, and I said, "See? I'm still alive! It's okay to make mistakes."

This shy boy took to heart what I said about practicing and quickly lost his reserve. His English improved hugely, and he became an enthusiast to the extent that six weeks later it was difficult to shut him up.

The regime of study at Beida goes like this—Classes begin at 8:00 a.m., and they go until 6:00, 7:00, 8:00, or 9:00 p.m. Six days a week. And then the kids come to rehearse a play. At this point an activity they did for fun—actually the same fun that they pay you with in grown-up theater—not credit, as at that time there was no theater department at Beida. Rashly, I offered extra coaching two mornings a week. Bunches of kids showed up at 7:00 a.m. in the coffee bar, where other bunches of kids bitten with the theater bug would be engaged in extracurricular play reading—texts like *Dr. Faustus, The Duchess of Malfi, Tis Pity She's A Whore*—light stuff like that. The Chinese work ethic begins somewhere on the other side of the Great Wall, a distance beyond that of the West.

I fell in love with the students.

It wasn't hard to do. They were shining examples of what human beings can be. Adjectives that apply are studious, diligent, courteous, attentive, aspiring, receptive, intelligent, civilized, and sweet. I could go on.

Except, of course, the children of the new middle class. They were easy to spot; they were the ones playing on their phones during lessons, and there are more of them each day as China rushes from the affliction of terrible poverty to the opposite one of wealth-beyond-the-dreams-of-avarice. One day soon, the classrooms in China will be as full of entitlement as those of the United States.

But that day is not yet. Joe told me a story about four Mongolian college students who took a train for three days and three nights from Mongolia to come to Beijing and find him. They came to ask him to help them with Shakespeare. He agreed to meet them in a cafe at around midnight. "I was shattered by the experience of their genuineness and beauty." he said.

He wrote a poetic monologue about the experience. Here's an excerpt:

The kid who plays King Henry holds up a sheaf of paper
And asks, 'We know this is most important.
Would you please now tell us
What it does mean?'
I take the ragged papers and read.

It is the Salique speech from Henry V,
I think, 'Who knows what the hell it means?

Oh God, kids, why didn't you
Choose something easy like Hamlet's fourth soliloquy,
Or the strangling scene in Othello, or Macbeth's dagger speech,
Or Cleopatra's death scene. Damn near anything
That at least makes some sort of sense.
But not the *&^%$# Salique speech!'

As I pause and wonder, King Henry speaks
'It is our deepest honor to meet you.
We know you know Shakespeare.
Will you help us to understand?'

My eyes, as often they do in China,
Fill up watery and red.
I am once again undone.
In the vast, wonderful presence of genuine humility.
'Will you help us to understand?'
Echoes above the breaking of my too-oft-broken heart.

They wonder at my tears.
I cannot stop them falling.
I am not embarrassed,
Nor do they seem so.
Puzzled maybe, and yet still most tender.

"Mistress Quickly asks,
'Are you sad?'
'I am happy', I say.

I wipe my nose and offer,
'Tomorrow we will learn all that I know
Of what these words in Henry V mean.
But tonight I tell you that a part of what they
Mean is this:

'In all the ways of hurt and sickness, of pain and death
Of convolutions and confusions
Of answerless questions and stinging, inexplicable rejections
That the twisted, twisting world has to offer,
Sometimes four people of peace and harmony
Come three days and nights from Mongolia;
Come with torn, dog-eared Shakespeare pages;
Come with pristine souls glowing;
Come with questions that give great answers in the asking;
And coming thus to be taught,
Teach rather.'

My friend and colleague Joe Graves naturally features a lot in this tale. He is one of the wilder theater people I have known, which is saying something. An infuriating type who can eat junk food by the bushel, drink black coffee by the quart and maintain a metabolism that gives him an apparently limitless capacity for work. He writes, teaches, directs, produces and acts. But after more than a decade in Beijing he still can't speak Chinese.

One time we were sitting in the Paradise coffee bar in the center of the Beida campus. The place was packed. We were chatting about the curious hybrid of post-Soviet control and the make-it-up-as-you-go of the Wild East. A condition that can make it difficult to navigate a developing theatrical enterprise.

"So why are you doing this?" I asked him, referring to his whole Chinese endeavor, and the impressive body of work he has accomplished there.

"Because it can't be done," he said.

In a pocket of the Beida campus hidden by trees, donated by the Spanish Embassy, there stands a statue of Don Miguel de Cervantes, who said, "Only one who attempts the absurd can achieve the impossible."

"You're a smart man, Joe," I said. "Why don't you learn the language?"

Joe went silent, the swoops and staccato cadences of spoken Chinese surrounding us, sounding now like the fluting of birds, now like the barking of a parade-ground sergeant.

"See?" he said. "I love the sound of it. I couldn't bear it if it turned out to be the same old bullshit!"

Which it is. Do you suppose that people who speak other languages sit there thinking how exotic they're sounding? No, they're wondering if there's time to do the washing, or if the hot guy or the hot girl in the English class noticed them, of course.

Talking of language:

When Joe had not been long in Beijing. He started giving classes, in English, on acting, theater history and Shakespeare. Most of the students were enthusiastic and responsive. This was new and interesting.

Except for one.

This one girl seemed resentful. More than that, she seemed to dislike Joe intensely, even to hate him. She exuded negativity.

Although I think many people who know him would agree when I characterize Joe as a kindly man, he's only human. Even though he tried everything he could to coax her into working on her English, and to try the acting exercises, bit by bit he began to also dislike her, and to dread trying to teach her, so intense and unpleasant was her resistance.

One day he gave an exercise to write one page of script in English and read it aloud. The turn came around to the hating girl. She came forward, and half way to the front she thrust the page at Joe, saying in broken speech, "You read it, you...you." Then she burst into tears

Joe took the paper and read.

It told how this girl was born in the poorest part of southern China. Her parents died when she was still an infant and she was raised by her grandmother. They were terribly poor, sometimes there was no food. They certainly had no television.

One day a neighbor acquired a TV and invited the girl and her grandmother to come and watch something. It was a program about an American multi millionaire, a billionaire actually. He was building a new home, one of several. The show told how the billionaire spent four million dollars on the door to this house. That was a day when the girl and her grandmother had not been able to eat.

There and then, the grandmother made the girl promise to learn English, because she thought it would be a way out of the third world. The girl promised. Secretly though, she swore to herself that she would never speak this language of greed.

"But," said the writing on the page, "you have been so gentle and kind to me..."

Of course, Joe's dislike of the girl dissolved instantly, and his heart filled with compassion.

The writing told how she had made the train journey at the weekend just passed—a very long journey—and had visited her grandmother, and there, on the stones of her grave, told her that she had lied about her intention to learn English, but that now she would change all that because now she knew she had been wrong to do so.

The page finished, "... if you will keep helping me and continue trying to teach me, I promise I will learn as well as I can, and if I ever become rich, I will buy you a Great Big Door."

It may even be an advantage to Joe that he does not speak Chinese, engaged as he frequently is in cutting theatrical deals. Theater business terms are nothing if not negotiable. Things adjust according to the variables of risk, celebrity, and popularity. A Westerner doing business in China enters a different paradigm. It is a truism to say that in China a contract is looked on as a point of view—it's just a suggestion. Business meetings are filled with the sounds of acquiescence. There is a social and commercial tradition, evolved over millennia of complex formal courtesy threaded through with the imperative of neither losing face oneself, nor causing another to lose it. This means that the word "yes" is used frequently. And here misunderstandings can arise. Typically, "yes" means, "Yes, we understand that is what you want." It does not always mean, "Yes, we agree to these terms."

The finer points of the contract for our theater were discussed in meetings that Joe attended and of which he understood not a word. Meanwhile, we rehearsed at night, and sometimes far into the night, those being the only hours we could get the whole cast together. One night somewhere in the small hours, an elderly Chinese scholar whom Joe had persuaded to take a small role, began to weep. Joe asked what was wrong.

He said, "They took my books, they took my books...and now I'm allowed to say the words of the greatest dramatist who ever lived. In my own country."

Our final *King Lear* rehearsal in the Democracy Building ended at midnight. The cast was dismissed to go and sleep. We were to return at ten in the morning. I went into the Beijing night with its Dickensian air. I was staying in an apartment some four miles from the campus. Usually I made the trip by bus, a ride that explains why contact sports are not necessary in China. The bus route traveled wide thoroughfares lined with giant institutions in functionalist architecture, punctuated by shopping malls that testify to advancing global monoculture—on every third or forth corner a Starbucks, or a KFC, certainly a McDonald's and the French supermarket chain Carrefour.

That night I splashed out on a taxi. The driver ducked his Volkswagen down a side lane I had not seen before and I had a glimpse of the backstage of Beijing itself. We went at high speed down a narrow two-lane street, dodging children and animals and oncoming vehicles of all kinds. Workshops and food shops were still active, and there were people all about. The chemically laden air and the fires burning in makeshift stoves cast strange lights and colors before us, and then the driver ducked again, and we were back on the front-cloth of the highway.

For a show the size of the *King Lear that* we did in Beijing in 2008, a three-day technical rehearsal would have been about right, preceded by a two-day get-in when the lights would have been focused and the stage assembled, the work being done by an experienced team of stagehands under the direction of an accomplished stage manager, with a production manager in attendance. That's the kind of thing that happens where I come from.

In contrast, the stage was completely bare when Joe and his eight apprentices came in at midnight. Working through the night, they built a frame to support a steeply raked playing area, hung flying pieces, and reorganized the lighting grid. They achieved all this by dawn. And the remaining daylight hours to curtain that night were given to technically rehearse all the cues for the running of the show. As I say, a process that normally—by which I mean in the West—takes three long days.

I came to work in the morning to find Joe in a state of excitement, pacing the back of the orchestra stalls in Centennial Hall, where we were to open that night. Doing double duty as both director and lead actor, he'd been up all night supervising everything. But he cast aside any fatigue and reminded me that what we do is not really work—it's play.

Our set was an ingenious series of long hanging cloths suspended from tracks high above the stage. These long strips of fabric could be moved into different configurations to create various environments. The fabric was painted with Chinese motifs, and under lighting it looked by turns courtly, chaotic, alarming and orderly. In the battle scenes it created a devastated landscape. One detail of stagecraft had been overlooked. The long canvas strips had not been sealed. When I started in theater there was a gluelike solution called size used to seal the canvas flats—and it has an aroma that for me always means backstage. But no one knew of it here. The consequence was that after a few performances, a fine rain of metallic paint fragments covered the stage. Toxic for sure—but no more so than the air outside.

In the backstage gloom I fell into conversation with a boy playing one of Lear's attendants. Robbie spoke fluent English with an accent. He asked me what I was going to do next. I told him I was about to play the German philosopher Martin Heidegger in a new play. Robbie became interested.

Small digression here. Remember how Arkansas and Sherlock led to *King Lear* in Beijing? Now here's a funny thing, while I was in Beijing that first time, my American cell phone would not work. Except just once. I remember clearly when it rang. I was in my studio apartment in Lin Da Bei Lu. The walls were covered with a storyboard for a novel I was trying to write, and I was living clichéd scenes from a writer's life, standing there tearing at my hair and making sounds like a caged animal—softly so, I was in a foreign country, after all. It was somewhere in the small hours of the night, and I knew that I should call it quits and sleep. Then the phone rang. I was surprised, it had been silent. But I was astonished when I heard Deborah Sherman, one of nature's protean theatrical firebrands, and producing artistic director of The Promethean Theatre in Florida, say, "I've got a play about Martin Heidegger. And the girl playing Hannah Arendt—she's crazy good." Well you can't ignore stuff like that. I agreed to do the show on the spot. Which is a good thing, because otherwise I wouldn't have met the fabulous Amy McKenna, who, fabulous though she is, plays no further part in this story.

Meanwhile backstage in Beijing, Robbie said, "Ah! I am a philosophy major."

The kid knew all the major European philosophers from Kant to Hegel to Swedenborg to Bertrand Russell. He'd read all the major works up to and including Sartre's *Being and Nothingness* and Heidegger's *On Being*. I only know these names and titles because, as part of my preparation to play Martin Heidegger, I read a charming volume called *How to Bluff Your Way in Philosophy*. We quickly reached the limits of what I could sensibly talk about, so I changed the subject.

I asked, "Do you think theater can be a force for political change?"

This brilliant, highly educated young man gave an immediate and confident answer. "No!" he said. He explained to me, somewhat as though he were dealing with a person of low intelligence, that theater is just "stories", and as such it has no meaning in the real world.

All that long day Joe was everywhere, checking lights and sound levels, springing up and down from the stage to work scenes. His energy was inexhaustible, as it can be when someone is doing what he loves most. At one point we were waiting stage right when the young Chinese beauty playing Cordelia halted her long entrance.

"Joe," she called over. "Where is my entrance music?"

"Er, Sophie," Joe said, using her English name. "You don't have any entrance music."

The beautiful girl suddenly realized the implications of what she had said. Watching from the wings it was a delicious and endearing example of an actor seeking focus. In the gloom I whispered to Joe, "It's nice to see that diva behavior is international."

"Yes," he agreed. "That would probably get you an equity card in the States."

The show was to begin at 7:00 p.m. At 6.40 p.m. we finished the final cue. With twenty minutes to curtain, I asked Joe if he wanted me to get him some coffee. At this point he had been on his feet and working without a break for about thirty-six hours. It was the one time in our acquaintance I ever saw him less than poised. He looked at me with a face more suited to Richard III at his vilest. "Oh come on," I said. "It's not as if you're just about to play Lear or anything…oh, wait a minute."

We performed in the Centennial Hall in the middle of the campus of Beida, a 2,800-seat theater. We performed in English with supra titles. A Chinese professor spoke to the audience for fifteen minutes beforehand. The silence during the show was either deep fascination or total bafflement. Likely some of both. But the response at the end was wildly enthusiastic.

After the show we all staggered away to take a late-night supper of *gong bao ji ding*—chicken with cashews. An ample plate of this tasty dish in a canteen-type, no-frills restaurant under fluorescent lights goes for twelve kuai—a little under two dollars at today's prices.

How strange was it to do one of Shakespeare's mightiest plays in Beijing? Quite strange, and then not so much. The story of *King Lear* is a familial one, and there's a love of story in China. The incongruity of young Asian actors grappling with Shakespearean text in English faded in a matter of minutes.

Joe showed me a video containing an impressive scene. There's an English lesson in *Henry V*. Shakespeare wrote the scene in French. The two young Chinese actresses spoke a local dialect. They also spoke Mandarin. They spoke English too, but not French. They learnt the scene phonetically!

The year after *King Lear* I went back to Beijing, and I taught English for a term at Beida, directing the undergraduates in an all-female *Julius Caesar*, and as the saying goes, "It seems so obvious, doesn't it? Surely just a question of who got there first." There were twenty-two girls in our production. Chinese society is traditionally non-expressive. It is a virtue to keep your feelings hidden, especially from people you do not know well. So I really had no idea whether the girls were enjoying the experience until one day the stage manager told me, "Our actresses are very excited."

One of the girls introduced me to her parents and I said in entry-level mandarin, *"Ni men de nu er shi yi ge hen hao de yan yuan."* : "Your daughter is a very good actress."

It was quite wonderful to see the look of pride and pleasure on the faces of people for whom seeing a play, let alone being in one, was unthinkable at one time.

Later in the same year I went to Hong Kong answering an invitation to guest as a judge on the panel of the Chinese University of Hong Kong's Shakespeare Festival. This was an event where universities from all over mainland China would submit a boiled down version of a Shakespeare play or even just a selection of scenes. They were limited to just three actors and twenty minutes. The first prize was a week in London, and a week in Stratford Upon Avon. What was it like? It was breathtaking. What they achieved was remarkable.

The whole thing was underwritten by two Hong Kong businessmen. One of them, Richard Liu was a genial, enthusiastic man. I asked him how he came up with this idea. We were on the 34th floor of the Raffles Hotel to attend a banquet that he gave. Looking over the sweep of the Hong Kong harbor, as dazzling a view by night as can be found, and suddenly taken by the incongruity of it all, I was lost in admiration for his support of this singular event.

Corporate cultural exchange has been facilitated, hence the large number of American fast-food outlets and other franchises with purchase in China. But what does it mean for actual culture? Specifically for theater? One thing you won't find in theaters in China is living playwrights discussing issues like degradation of the environment, exploitation of the workers, freedom of the press, and manipulation of currency. But the authorities in China have nothing to fear from theater. Look what happens in the West when a high status playwright gives us a play which decries the false politics that took us to war? David Hare wrote a play called "Stuff Happens". It played to sold out houses in Britain, the USA, and Australia. Did it have the slightest impact on policy?

For enlightened social commentary we must turn to Shakespeare.

Zhu Shenghao is China's principal translator of Shakespeare. He was a young man in Shanghai in the 1930s. He translated some eight or nine of Shakespeare's plays—then the Japanese invaded, and the office where he worked was torched. His work was lost. He began again, and this time he translated more than twenty of the thirty-seven Shakespeare plays. He encountered the invading

Japanese a second time, and a second time they destroyed his work.

With his wife Song Qiru, he fled to a remote village in the east of China, and for the last years of his life he lived in extreme poverty until his death from tuberculosis, aged thirty-two. Zhu Shenghao died with his pen in his hand. The last words to pass his lips were, "Once more unto the breach, dear friends, once more." At that time he had completed thirty-one and a half translations of Shakespeare's plays.

Shakespeare is esteemed in China. And the authorities allow Shakespearean productions, which talk of so many human conditions in ways that modern writers may not. In *Henry V*, the Duke of Burgundy appeals that, "Peace, dear nurse of arts, plenties and joyful births..." be given a chance. I don't know about China, but anytime I hear the more belligerent politicians of the West bravely committing other people's children to go to war, I wish that they were required to learn by heart the Duke of Burgundy's entire speech, and recite it publicly on television. Was it political of Shakespeare to write a speech like that? Is it political to quote it here?

If it is, please don't tell my friend the lady at the visa counter in the Chinese consulate in New York.

The Middle Kingdom Looms

Year of the Rat is one of Roy Smiles's best plays.

In 2011, about nine months before the London Olympics, I was in Minneapolis, Minnesota, USA. I was talking with Joe in China via Skype. He mentioned a play about George Orwell and suggested that we do it Beijing. I wasn't sure, seeing as Orwell was famously anti totalitarian, but I knew the playwright, having been in *Ying Tong* (the play about the Goons) in Philadelphia—so I facebooked Roy, who was in London, and asked him if we could have the rights to *Year of the Rat*. Within four minutes Roy had replied to me, saying he liked the idea, and he sent me a script. I emailed it to Joe in China. Round trip Beijing to Minneapolis to London in ten minutes with a possible production.

I was at the Guthrie rehearsing *Charley's Aunt*. When I was twelve years old I was taken to see *"The Aunt"* as some call it, in London. I knew I wanted to be an actor, and this was a matinee that opened a door to the world I wanted to be a part of. I laughed till my face hurt. I had never heard hundreds of people all laughing together before. I thought it was a brilliant sound. We were taken backstage and I was introduced to the man then playing the old fart, Wolfe Morris. Years later one of my friends got together with his daughter—both of them actors—and forty years later I came to play that same part. Small world, huh?

I liked this international quick-tech communication from the middle of the continental United States. Joe called me again a couple of days later and said, "I've met a Chinese producer who wants to do a Peking Opera version of *Timon of Athens* in London."

This was an incongruity moment. The first of many.

It probably wouldn't hurt to insert a Shakespearean prologue here.

One of those ones that says how although the story all looks pretty straightforward with the Earl of such and such wanting to bed the Duke of so and so's daughter, and even though the boys down at the Hedgehog Tavern are still quaffing the ale, and the women in the play are the smartest characters anyway, even though played by boys, hold on ladies and gentlemen in the audience, because there's going to be some complicated plot action in act V.

Or, I suppose I could say, "You know how it is when you read a Russian novel?"

"Pass the samovar Ivan Romanitch."

"Of course Ilya Ilyitchkavitch."

What I'm getting at is that there will be quite a few characters with names unfamiliar to a Western reader, and the story does get a bit involved at about two thirds of the way through this book. I'd go so far as to say that it did actually get rather more involved than I will describe, having confined myself to a cherry-picked, creative fictional account. So much so, that I had trouble keeping track myself.

Of course I had no idea of what was to come at the point of this Skype call in the middle of the continental USA. So I said, "That sounds wild." And I agreed to look around for a theater for this interesting project.

Timon of Athens, Peking Opera style, would run during the London Olympics. After a week's brisk telephoning I was able to offer three London venues ranging in size (and hire fee) to my friend Joe's Beijing producer. At which point I was introduced to her by phone.

Xi Li was a person of energy and determination. She had worked in the United States, and she spoke fluent, but not perfect English. I explained what I had found, talked through the size of the venues, the location, the basic prices and some of the implications. And I said, "Of course, it is the Olympics."

"Right!" said Xi Li.

When I spoke to Rosie Johnson, the chief executive at Hoxton Empire, on Xi Li's behalf, I explained that part of the project was a feel-good initiative. We talked about how the previous Olympic Games had been in Beijing and now they were in London, and we discussed cultural exchange and the friendship between our two countries. I got more information about rates and charges. I passed all this back to Xi Li. A contract was issued.

We talked about how to find an audience for the show, and I said, "Well, it is the Olympics. It might be a little difficult."

"We'll get one," said Xi Li. She sounded confident.

"And there will be lots of extra charges."

"No problem."

Hoxton Empire is a late Victorian theater and the distinctive horseshoe shape of the auditorium makes for an incredible acoustic.

A month went by. I received a phone call. It was Xi Li. "Colin!"

"Hello?" I said.

There was a change of program.

"We're not going to do *Timon of Athens*," Xi Li said, "we're going to do *The Blind Men and the Elephant*!"

"Oh?"

I was surprised. Joe was slated to direct, and I had received a script of the Peking Opera's *Timon of Athens*, titled *Cash*. There were some interesting photographs. This was a change of direction. I called Joe.

"I hear you're doing *The Blind Men and the Elephant* instead of *Cash*," I said.

"Oh?" said Joe.

"You didn't know?"

"Um, no."

At this point I considered withdrawing from the project, seeing as the man who had introduced me had been given the elbow without his knowledge. But Joe said, "Stick around, why not? It could be interesting."

So I called the Hoxton Empire. And I explained that *The Blind Men and the Elephant* is a traditional Chinese folktale very popular in China, and it appears in many guises there.

"Ok," said Rosie. "Maybe that's even more interesting. I wasn't quite sure how to sell a Peking Opera version of *Timon of Athens*."

Xi Li called me not long before Christmas. Change was in the air.

"Colin! We're not going to do *The Blind Men and the Elephant*! We're going to do a new show about a secret recipe. We call it *Gong Fu Spaghetti Pie*."

"How about *Enchanted Lunch*?"

"No!" said Xi Li. "We call it *Gong Fu Spaghetti Pie!*"

"Xi Li," I said. "You're paying the bills. You call it whatever you like."

Rosie asked me a question. "Colin, what's going on?"

It was not the last time she would ask that. I assured her there would be absolutely no more changes.

The New Year began. There was a call from China, asking if I could now find accommodation for three hundred kids between the ages of ten and sixteen. I said the same two things I habitually said: "It's the Olympics. It will be expensive."

I fired up my Skype account and made many calls. Francine was an old friend from London, who had a connection to the London Borough of Camden, London's most leftist-leaning local authority. She had a word with the mayor, who was sympathetic to the project, and she agreed to release a school for our use. They would fit it with cots, security personnel, and the required chaperones. We talked about catering and transport. I told Xi Li.

"No, we don't need that any more," she said.

I canceled the arrangements and made the necessary apologies.

The next day Xi Li asked me to find accommodation for sixty-five Peking Opera actors.

Hotel prices in London were doubling on an hourly basis in Olympic anticipation fever. I couldn't go back to Camden, having used up my stock of good will there. I phoned around. Nobody would admit to having availability at prices connected with reality, but then I struck accommodation gold. Imperial University in central London could offer rooms, their students would be away for the summer..

Gong Fu Spaghetti Pie was put on sale. I came around to the title.

So I had a theatrical troupe from a communist country staying in a place called Imperial and performing at a place called Empire—what could go wrong?

From Minneapolis I went to West Palm Beach in Florida to act in a play called *The Pitmen Painters*.

A play about coalminers from the north-east of England, it originated in Newcastle, written by Lee Hall (the man who wrote *Billy Elliot*), transferred to the Royal National Theatre in London, then to the West End and then to Broadway. When a play gets that kind of pedigree it goes all over the American regions, and the playwright gets to cash in and enjoy what is likely an infrequent surplus.

To me it was counterintuitive that in such a monied locale our play would find an audience, but it went gangbusters. I wondered how themes of the trade unions and the self-improvement of the ordinary working man would play in the People's Republic of China. Weeks passed. It was now spring. I called my client in Beijing.

She told me there was a change of program.

We were now going to add a pop concert starring a fifteen-year-old girl from Guangzhou, a children's talent show with kids from all over China, an orchestral concert starring a glamorous Chinese soprano, and a troupe of Peking Opera actors performing *The Jade Palace*.

"What about *Gong Fu Spaghetti Pie*?" I asked.

"*Gong Fu Spaghetti Pie* is cut," said Xi Li.

I gleaned that Xi Li had sublet the hire period to people whom I had never heard of, and that instead of one set of technical production requirements, there would now be four. This would have implications.

"Colin!" said Rosie when I called her. "What's going on?"

Fair question. This would have been a good moment for me say, "Your guess is as good as mine," or "Don't ask me, I'm only the producer," or "Wouldn't I be a happy man if I knew that?"

But I didn't say any of that. Why not? Well, I was right behind the idea of the project. I think—all right, I thought then—that the more cultural exchange that can happen, the better it would be for world peace. It took a certain amount of persuasion before Rosie agreed to accommodate this transformation. In good faith I assured her that all the bills would be paid.

Other fun stuff that went down at this time included a request for an orchestra. I opened negotiations with one of London's top five, only to be told that one of Xi Li's sub-letters had procured an orchestra separately. Looking back, I see that at this point one of Shakespeare's "alarums and excursions" scenes should have played in my head.

I canceled the arrangements and made the necessary apologies.

Man of La Mancha

In May I went to China to take a look at a production of *Man of La Mancha* in which I was a prospective investor. It had been three years since I was in Beijing. But I had been in regular contact with Joe Graves, and month after month we had discussed and dreamed many versions of a plan to finance various productions.

"How are things going with Xi Li?" he asked.

"If I ever do this again," I said, thinking of the confusion that was developing, "there are a lot of things I will try to pin down in advance."

"Yes," said Joe. "And you know what? It will all be exactly the same."

A lot was the same in Beijing, but more of it. More subways (many more), more trees, more buildings, more people—African visitors among them (there had been none there in 2009)—and more money required to get through a day. That is, if like me, you enjoy Western comforts such as decent coffee.

I met Xi Li in person. It was impossible not to warm to her. She had the charisma and charm common both to driven business people and to theatrical stars, that ability to focus on you exclusively and make you feel as if you are the only person who matters. She was small of stature, with a ready laugh and smile, and plenty of impish humor. She took me on a long drive through Beijing traffic to see a children's show her company was presenting. The theater was packed. The kids giggled constantly at the silly japes and the monsters that would appear from behind bushes. Xi Li was sensitive about the quality of the piece. "Room for improvement?" she asked as she introduced me to the director.

"Hen hao wanr," I said in my best Beijing accent, "A lot of fun."

And it was. All right, the technical side could have tightened up a little, but when a couple of hundred kids squeal in delight, what's wrong with that?

There was a political vibe going on in the city at large. We were in May, but in November— oddly right about the time of the US elections— a change of government leadership was due to occur. President Hu would be leaving, and President Xi (no relation to my client) would succeed him. People wondered what the new leader would mean. Was the man a liberal or a conservative? A reformer or a hardliner?

Anything offered for the public view in China, such as a play, has to be approved by the authorities. The coming change meant that official permission was taking longer to come by. As well as this, the government had announced that for the month of October, just before the leadership change, it would commandeer any theater at a moment's notice if it needed a venue to hold a meeting. It was not the time to challenge governmental cultural tolerance levels with plays such as *Year of the Rat*. These conditions affected and delayed plans that Joe and I had made. But we thought that *Man of La Mancha* couldn't possibly be objectionable to anyone, so we went ahead with the production, in which I was now something approaching a consultant associate, with a view to becoming a co-producer later on.

As with my first visit in 2008, my planned accommodation had fallen through. Logistics in the Middle Kingdom are nothing if not changeable. Joe found me a distant apartment, which I shared with an agreeable American named Dan. Dan was a theater practitioner of the old New York style—by which I mean he'd been at the famous Actor's Studio, where he'd studied with Bill Hickey. Now he taught acting and directing in California. He was a large man, well over six feet tall, and his carriage had the easy grace of a longtime practitioner of Tai Chi, in which discipline he was quite an expert. You see Tai Chi practiced all over in Beijing. Dan thought the purest forms were now available in the West. The kids in our show called him Big Panda.

Dan was playing the Innkeeper. I agreed to guest for a few performances with a cameo as the

Captain of the Guard—the role that opens the show—delivering Cervantes to prison. When I was twenty-one, and ambition for acting was all I knew, I heard a man about the age I am now say grateful words that his role was small. I was baffled then, but I get it now, especially if, as it often is, the money is the same no matter how many words you say. When Joe talked me into doing it, I said, "Hmm, get in, get out. My kind of part."

The apartment was in a suburb called Xi Er Qi; it was two long stops from Wudaokou, the trendy student hangout, which was a twenty-minute walk from Beijing University. Wudaokou has bars and restaurants and a twenty-four-hour cafe with reliable Internet connectivity, decent coffee, and Western food. Xi Er Qi, not so much. We were on the tenth floor of a twenty-story building in a small grouping of similar towers. I could see the subway station from my window most mornings, but usually not the small mountains rising in the distance. The air was viscous, so opaque as to make distance viewing impossible. Dan had a hacking cough most of the time he was in Beijing. He made the mistake of breathing. Silly man, I could have told him not to do that.

Fences surrounded the apartment buildings in Xi Er Qi, and you entered through a gate. At the gate there was a small group of single-story buildings that perhaps had once been offices. Hard to say because they were in a state of semi-demolition. Someone had been in there and taken a sledgehammer to the roofs and the walls and then stopped just as soon as there was enough rubble to make the place unusable.

Except it wasn't. In the evenings vendors of street food would arrive and set up small barbecues along the curbside, and they put tables and chairs in the shallows of the debris. And in this war-zone backdrop people would dine. Skewers of lamb chunks were a single kuai, fifteen cents at today's prices, and they'd be ordered in batches of ten with bottles of Tsingdao beer, China's finest export. Dan and I, returning from rehearsal, would walk through these makeshift dining salons. Even though Beijing hosts many foreigners—half a million by one count—in Xi Er Qi we were unusual on the skyline.

I had persisted with an irregular study of Mandarin to the extent that I could now say, *"Zhe zhende shi ji rou ma?"*:"Is this really chicken?" At this point, deterred by an episode of Chairman's Revenge, I was staying away from the street food, but here I tried a skewer—tasty!

When Dan's cough wasn't hacking the airwaves, he and I would chat as theater veterans. We agreed on the basics—that vocational theater practitioners take a vow of poverty, that celebrity obsession distorts the profession, that it's tough at the top, the bottom, and the middle, tough all the way through in fact. And then Dan said something so sensible, and so important, that I am going to record it here.

He said, "But there is no substitute for owning your own soul."

The apartment was functional. A living room and a kitchen. The beds were comfortable. There was air conditioning that we sometimes used—it did almost take the edge off the sweltering heat. The shower drained into a hole in the floor. There was a washing machine, and a small china figurine of the Chairman himself was the centerpiece of a collection of knick-knacks on some bookshelves—no books. The Internet connectivity was reliable only in Dan's room.

I did a lot of early-morning subway rides to Wudaokou to go to the Internet cafe, which was open twenty-four hours a day and where I could get connected and make calls to London. The production there was approaching, and questions were being asked. Internet connectivity is ragtime in Beijing, and you can't get YouTube, Facebook, and Google. This is mildly annoying, and you've got to wonder what the authorities are afraid of—that people might start thinking for themselves? And why do the rulers bother? In any case, it's a minor inconvenience; there's plenty of software that can get around the restrictions.

It suited me to rise early. The first subway in Beijing starts at 5:30 a.m., and it's the best time to ride, but even then don't expect a seat. Millions of people use the Beijing subway every day, and a ride to any destination in that vast city costs two kuai—a sensible thirty-five cents, or twenty UK pence—seems like the right sort of price to me.

First the travelers pass their bags through the ubiquitous security machines, then they line up in orderly rows along yellow lines painted on the platforms, perpendicular to the doors. The arriving passengers disembark along an invisible middle line, and when they've left, the new passengers get on. In theory. In practice three or four people stumble off the train, and then the waiting lines which have been neat hitherto surge forward. At that point a New York-style scrum occurs as the passengers moving in opposite directions try to pass their bodies through one another instead of around each other. The embarking commuters are pressed and stacked into the trains by human packers dressed in bright yellow, who keep an aggressive motivational commentary going the whole time. Once I was caught in the zenith of the rush-hour crush. The pressure was hydraulic.

We rehearsed *Man of La Mancha* in the Democracy Building on the Beida campus in the evenings. It was like old times. Except the Lady Keeper of the Door was no longer around. We got inside every evening without a fuss. *Man of La Mancha* was a good play to be practicing at Beida, given the statue of Cervantes in the bushes.

The cast was Dan and me and Joe, doing his frequent gig as director and lead actor, and the usual assortment of talented, handsome Chinese kids. I say, "usual" because most of the kids I met in China seemed to be abundantly both of these things. Some of the cast members were professionals, and about half of them were students new to drama. There was a standout performer—a graduate of the Shanghai Music Conservatory. In her mid twenties, her English name was Nine, as in the number nine. She played Aldonza. Wow! This girl could sing. Passionately!

I went to open a bank account in preparation for the slate of projects that Joe and I planned to undertake. I was recommended to go to Guo Mao, the Central Business District. A spotless environment, hi-tech, with steel, glass, chrome and marble-facing on every surface. This was the showpiece front-cloth of Beijing, Singapore-sterile. Even the dust was banished, and there was no one hawking phlegm in the streets. I gained a visitor pass and took the elevator which moved with a whisper to the eighteenth floor—of about fifty floors in the building. The Bank of China had a large corner office with panoramic views and was staffed by charming, elegant young men and women.

"Can I open an account?" I asked.

"Yes, of course. Fill in this form and take a seat," said the woman.

It was all done with exquisite etiquette, in impeccable English. A few minutes later I was shepherded to a counter, and another elegant—I want to say "chick" rather than "young woman" because she was fashion-model glamorous—started inputting data into a computer. The mood couldn't have been friendlier. I started congratulating myself on my contribution to international relations and a moment later the classy chick behind the glass, and bear in mind that I had handed over my passport at this point, said, "!!??"

She swiveled the monitor so that the classy chick who was assisting me—yes, she was runway material as well—could see it. Then she said, "!!??"

The monitor was swiveled away again. There was a beat, and the two Chinese chicks stared at each other.

"Is something wrong?" I said.

Beat.

"There is a problem with the system." said one.

Minutes passed. My passport was passed around among various people behind the glass, each now looking less glamorous to me than the one before, but each with the same response to whatever it was they saw on the monitor, "!!!???"

Finally, about fifteen minutes into this thing—a long fifteen minutes—a suave guy, but no great looker, came along and said to me, "You are on a blacklist."

And then I said, "!!!???"

Another fifteen minutes passed. No one was talking English now, instead, there was some rapid Chinese. A soldier walked around flourishing a truncheon. I reached for my phone, thinking I'd better use it before I was hauled off to some distant province and given a bit of electrical re-education. I wondered if the phrase "Chinese water torture" still applied now that the West has adapted it in the name of Freedom.

I called Joe and, trying hard to keep the jumpiness out of my voice, explained that we might be on the verge of a spot of bother. His reply did nothing to calm my nerves.

"Well, whatever you do," he said, "for fuck's sake keep my name out of it!"

This was our short-hand humor, and normally I would have laughed.

Another ten minutes passed, and then suddenly everyone was speaking English again. The suave guy re-appeared and told me, "There was a mistake."

Suddenly the guy looked to me like something on a cover of GQ. It was all smiles now, and I opened the account. I staggered out of there, maintaining the sangfroid for which the British are so justly famed. Dazed by the experience, I went for a calming cup of coffee at a cafe on one of the boulevards where I had a ringside view of the astonishing traffic.

The Beijing subway system has taken millions off the roads but now more and more people buy cars, so those few vacant spots in the traffic stream fill up fast. The re-instated anti-congestion measure of only allowing odd-number-plated cars to drive on days when even-numbered ones don't has gone another step to reduce congestion. Xi Li had an American solution to any possible inconvenience: two cars.

Still, I reflected as the caffeine took effect, Beijing coffee has improved beyond recognition. Maybe they'll work on the air next.

Since I'd arrived in Beijing I was in daily contact with Xi Li's office as even more ideas about the coming London season flowed through. We discussed merchandising, branding and a possible London exhibition of Chinese art. I also met with certain associates and intermediaries, including Chen Ling who was the company's formidable financial comptroller. She was unusually tall, power-dressed, with a demeanor than meant business.

Xi Li herself was an exciting person to know. Although short in stature, she had energy enough to run three or four bodies of that size. She could generate mounds of ideas on present and future projects. I liked her a lot, and it was always interesting talking with her. I liked her so much, that were it not heresy to say so in China—official policy denying millennia of sophisticated religious thought—I could have considered that we had been friends in a past life.

As one who thinks that having some theater around is a very good thing for a society, I was impressed with what Xi Li was doing for her country. She was well placed to be at the forefront of the current gold rush to culture that is going on in China, and I hoped that we could collaborate on future projects. This was why I stayed to the end, and also why I was so absurdly accommodating in my approach—naive on my part, but there it is.

I suggested to Xi Li that maybe I should talk with the director of each of the four teams going to London. She told me, "The man who waits, travels swiftly towards the goal."

All very true no doubt, but a bit taoist for my Western sensibility.

However, I reflected, social signals are different in different cultures. In New York for example, every seventh person is an entrepreneurial self-starter and there's always a performance or an exhibition somewhere below Fourteenth Street.

Suppose you're one of these types and you're trying to get people to come along to your event. If someone says, "I'll try to make it,"—in New York speak that means, "I'm not coming." Along these lines there were social codes at work in Beijing that I did not understand.

Still, if I were going to produce the various shows, it would make sense for me to be directly in touch with each group. Wouldn't it?

Man of La Mancha came to production week.

It had been a highly mobile season for me so far. New York to Los Angeles, then to Australia—I was doing a lot of air travel anyway, and I have family there, so a quick detour to see them seemed to be a good idea—and then Beijing. I was looking forward to a few weeks of theater routine, and I wanted the traveling to stop. But the daily mobility continued at a local level. The Trojan House Theatre—yes, "House" not "Horse"—was a ninety-minute subway ride from Xi Er Qi in northwest Beijing to the trendy, arty Chao Yang district in the southeast. Dan made a good joke once as we travelled to the theater.

"Two Chinamen get on a subway and sit down!"

President Hu had made a keynote speech earlier in the year—reported in the *New York Times*—which had decried the invasion of Western culture in China. Traveling by subway across the one-hundred-mile diameter of China's capital city, watching the advertisements for first-world toys and candies displayed on the LED screens that line the subway walls, you have to think that Mr. Hu might have had a point.

"We must take the game to them!" said President Hu—well, not in exactly those words. But the next export on China's list is soft power in the form of culture. A rumor has started that China has decided to create a test cricket team within ten years. If this is true, and the form of the past three decades is anything to go by, they'll do it. It is the sports equivalent of President Kennedy announcing that America would put a man on the moon.

The Trojan House Theatre was an agreeably funky venue tucked several blocks behind a main thoroughfare, and along an alleyway. It was in a designated arts district; there were boutique clothing stores, an art gallery, and a museum of modern art that sprouted a dozen statues of goblinesque figures sitting on its parapet a hundred feet up in the air.

The Trojan House had an internet cafe and a studio-type auditorium to seat maybe two hundred and fifty people with a thrust playing area on the flat. There were no actual dressing rooms, so a series of drapes were slung over wires, and we twenty-five actors all crowded into a space that could have comfortably seated six or seven. The Beijing dust was everywhere. Backstage is seldom pristine, this one set a new low. So what!? The best theater happens when passion, skill, and story converge. We had all that.

Man of La Mancha is a story about Miguel de Cervantes—a dreamer, aspirant, entrepreneur, soldier/poet, sometime tax collector and first-rank adventurer at large. And oh yes, he happened to write the most enduring comic novel of the mid last millennium, *Don Quixote*. The show has some catchy tunes, and Joe Graves, whose offstage character makes him excellent casting for Cervantes, gave an empathetic performance that touched people to the heart. And our Chinese supporting cast? There was a moment-to-moment quality in these young performers—it's something you can't fake and it's like gold dust on stage, so much so that one forgot the actual Beijing dust in every corner. And that girl who played Aldonza, the one whose English name was Nine, had a voice worth traveling the globe to hear.

Our first audiences were small. Our young Chinese producers were working on the fringes of the media systems, and they had little access to effective publicity. Theater criticism takes different forms in the great capitals of the world. In London, public opinion is shaped across half a dozen national papers. In New York, the *New York Times* has absolute sway. In Beijing, with our *Man of La Mancha*, a posse of people calling themselves journalists turned up, took the free drinks, and left at intermission.

I asked one of my Chinese colleagues to explain.

"We don't have any tradition," he told me. "You can pay someone to write a good review."

"Is that what you did?"

"No, we can't afford it."

I thought about *The New York Times* and its influence. I remember seeing a splendid production of *Suite in Three Keys* closed by a carelessly written review. Conversely, *The Times* wrote a love letter of praise for an opaque text given a production by the Atlantic Theatre in downtown Manhattan. The show sold out its run within forty-eight hours of publication.

The media is powerful, right? And propaganda on both sides of the Pacific pervades the airwaves and the print. There is a difference though—in China no one believes it, but in America the citizens insist on it.

I already knew that we had some success with this show that couldn't be measured in box-office receipts or press coverage. One of the young actors, whose role required him to listen to Cervantes more or less through the whole show, confided to me that he found it difficult to hear the same story every night. I gave the conventional advice a teacher of acting might pass along. "You've got to imagine it's the first time you're hearing it."

The kid was ahead of me. He said, "But at the end, I feel as if my heart has been washed."

Our Beijing audience built by word of mouth. We had the advantage that no one would read the local reviews, if indeed there were any, knowing them to be worthless from any objective standard. The audience built quickly, and by our third performance we were at 70 percent attendance. We were hopeful.

And then the authorities closed a show.

It was about a week after a bad incident in the Beijing streets. Mostly, Beijing feels pretty safe. You can walk around in the small hours of the morning, and no one bothers you. But some lowlife, drunken British guy had attacked a young Chinese girl in the street. Two Chinese youths had come to the rescue and beaten the crap out of the guy. The incident had been captured on closed-circuit TV, and the two youths had instantly gained hero status. The drunken Brit was living beyond his visa in Beijing. He was carted off to prison where, I imagine, he had an extremely rough time.

Another Western theater group in the city had opened a production of *Oklahoma* (that well-known piece of theatrical subversion), and the news came to us that one night the police had gone in and cleared out the audience. We were puzzled. No explanation could be found. The government then announced one hundred days of crackdowns on illegal immigrants in Beijing. Joe advised me to carry my passport everywhere in case I was stopped and papers demanded. The government was following the time-honored technique as advised by Shakespeare's *Henry IV* to "busy giddy minds with foreign quarrels." Works every time. Just ask the Americans.

All of a sudden, Xi Li invited me to a meeting with Long Shun, the director of the orchestral concert that would be number three in the lineup in London. He lived in Sanlitun—the Beijing equivalent of New York's West Village. The Xi Er Qi locale where I was staying was a millimeter thick in greasy grime. Long Shun's apartment was showcase-clean.

The soprano who would star in this concert attended the meeting with her people. Her name was Xiao Xue, and she was certainly one of the most beautiful women in China (where there is no shortage of beautiful women). Long Shun himself made the very good coffee. His designers were there too, and the composer and musical director. We were a dozen at the conference table, and there were assistants hovering, ready to brew the second batch of coffee. From 8:00 p.m. till near midnight we talked. Some smoked. The orchestra and the choir, the visiting local talent, the design concept and the filming were all discussed in detail and at length. Inevitably, LED screens were spoken of. The tone of the meeting was friendly and stimulating. Clearly everyone was an expert in his or her field and looking forward to working in London. This show would be a cultural showpiece, a high-end evening requiring some pricy equipment and manpower. Long Shun was treated with the sort of deference you would expect in the highest-level American boardroom.

At the end of the meeting I said, "We'll need a production manager."

No one took much notice.

We had moved a long way from a young company doing a Peking Opera version of a Shakespeare play.

Air Miles

I left the meeting in Sanlitun and called Joe. The London project had just gone up a couple of notches in production terms. We met in the early hours after midnight in Wudaokou. I explained that the productions shaping up in London were kind of complex—no publicity, delays in signing the contract (and therefore nothing on sale), complicated technical requirements, and an opacity about who was involved. I needed to go to London to get some arrangements in place.

Between May and September 2012 I did the kind of traveling usually only seen in action movie franchises. This was the itinerary: New York—Minneapolis—New York—Los Angeles—Sydney—Shanghai—Beijing—Chicago—New York—London—New York—Chicago—Beijing—Sydney—Los Angeles—New York—London—New York. That information may be more than needed to tell this story, but I'm just mentioning it, and I'd like to say that jet-lag takes us all in different ways.

Joe was peeved, but we agreed that I quit *Man of La Mancha*—one of the keen young Chinese actors would replace me.

I made the trek the long way around, via America. I must have been in the air somewhere over Chicago when the requests for letters of invitation started. There were procedures for sponsoring foreign visitors to the United Kingdom, and the venue knew how they worked, but our Chinese colleagues insisted that all that was needed was a letter of invitation listing people's names and passport numbers. As soon as I landed in New York I checked my email, and from the airport lounge I drafted a template letter that seemed to satisfy the bureaucracy on the Chinese end, and accordingly ten people were invited.

Then six of the names were changed, and the letters were reissued. Then three of the passport numbers were changed, and the letters were reissued a second time. Then there was an urgent request that the letters be express mailed to various parts of China. The following day another batch of letters of invitation for an additional twenty people was requested—this one equally urgent as the first. The letters were issued, and then the changes to names and passport numbers began, and the letters were reissued. Sometimes the physical letters made it all the way across the world, but sometimes the various postal services were not quite up the task and in the more remote regions the letters sometimes failed to turn up.

I took a layover in New York, and I had breakfast with one of my agents, Sam Silver. Sam was a keen young man. He told me that he was planning a round-China trip that would take him from Chongqing to Xian, to Lhasa, to Shenzhen, to Guanzhou, to Shanghai, Beijing and other places too. And off he went, traveling alone, just hopping on and off planes. His interest in the country was a surprise to me, and his intrepid journey was somewhat astonishing. It would have been impossible to even imagine such a trip when I was his age.

A couple of days later riding in a yellow cab, I looked back at the stalagmite skyline of the city that never sleeps. It was good to be back in the "Free World" as we who live there call it. The air, in the mellow Manhattan summer, was refreshingly breathable. Some of the streets of the West Village where I live still have cobblestones and many are lined with mature trees.

I hopped on a plane myself to go to London. The business with the letters of invitation continued for many weeks, and usually urgent requests would come for new letters or amended ones on a Friday afternoon between 4.30 p.m. and 5.30 p.m. With grace and patience, Julia, the PA to the Hoxton chief executive, would prepare the letters, scan them, email them and express snail-mail them. At which point, our colleagues in China would ask for changes to be made. It was confusing to say the least and none of us on the UK side were 100 percent confident that we were fulfilling the consular requirements. Julia expressed it eloquently, "Colin, this doesn't make any sense, but I'll do it anyway."

Another of Xi Li's sub-letter clients was a substantial media company in China, which had in turn subcontracted a raft of other service providers. There was a design team out of Hong Kong, there was some kind of procurement company out of Thailand, there was a middle-management company from Beijing, there were PR types from various parts of China, and there were marketing and PR people from London. Fluent marketing and public relations jargon was exchanged freely. It was a dialect that I found more challenging than Mandarin.

All of these new players were now contacting the London venue directly. They issued large, late, and immediate demands. The venue ignored them, having never heard of them and having no contractual relationship with any of them. My client was the only party they were in contract with. The new players were puzzled as to why they were being ignored.

As the UK producer on the project you might think that it would make sense for me to be fully informed as to who these people were and what their roles would be. That was what the venue expected. No such information from China was forthcoming. Requests for such information were interpreted as interference, and they were sidetracked. It was like…it was like…well, it was like doing business in China.

Which would have been fine except that we were doing business in the United Kingdom.

An issue of developing contention, that would play to the end of the entire gig in a big way, was that if the planned orchestral concert was to be filmed then a recording fee would have to be paid to the orchestra, and the theater technicians would get paid time and a half.

I dealt with the formidable Chen Ling on this issue. I explained the fees and charges.

She was appalled. "What? Even if they don't do anything?"

"It's not exactly nothing that they do," I said. "These are skilled people, and if you record the concert, you can exploit their expertise, and you can make money. The thinking is that it's only fair they should be compensated."

"Cut them out!" said Chen Ling. "Cut them out of the picture!"

"If there are cameras in the theater on the night of the concert, the musicians will sit there on the stage, as you have paid them to do, but they will not play their instruments, because you will not have paid them to do that."

Chen Ling was aghast. "I don't have the budget for this!"

I mentioned that this cost was among the extra charges I had tried to tell her about in one of our initial meetings. "I didn't listen to you!" was Chen Ling's reply.

"Colin," asked Rosie, "what's going on?"

It was not exactly easy to answer this question.

Because of the burgeoning complexity Hoxton Empire issued an addendum to the contract. The venue now required a substantial deposit against the labor costs they would incur during the production week. The new contractual terms required a qualified UK production manager to take responsibility for the local hiring of technical staff and equipment. The production manager would also prepare a schedule for the production week and the growing, complicated logistics.

I told Xi Li, about it. "Calm down!" she yelled.

The high-end Hong Kong design team, engaged to create the concert for the pop star, sent a sheaf of technical specifications that would have been about right for the Rolling Stones playing a concert in Hyde Park. "If you put this much lighting in the theater grid," said one of our technical guys, "you will melt the performers. And you will fuse the venue. There's not enough electricity in the building."

When I landed in London I met with Selena Smith, a possible production manager. She had wide experience in all aspects of stage production. I gave her a précis and engaged her services. The Olympics were coming, as I keep mentioning, and I was lucky to find her.

Xi Li did not agree.

I tried to explain that British theater is a highly regulated environment. There are health and safety procedures, union requirements, insurance requirements, and rules concerning copyright. There are few equivalents in the People's Republic, which is why as the costs were rolled out, my Chinese client was baffled. I would have done better, much better, to have smiled, said nothing, and allowed Xi Li to figure all that out—or not—for herself.

Xi Li sent a young Chinese guy to assist in the process. His name was Zhou Kim. He came to London under various highly imaginative titles: project manager, assistant production manager, and general coordinator. Zhou Kim had many sterling qualities. Among them were a truly charming smile and a tendency to say, "Yes, I understand" in moderately good English.

I had engaged a young Chinese lady living in London, named Molly, as an interpreter. She had studied event management and spoke fluent English. This should have been a useful move, because as I and my team, via Molly, explained our contractual obligations to Zhou Kim, he could explain them to Xi Li, and the other mystery participants, but these explanations did not happen. Does that sound like a basis for confusion? Right. But at least we had people in place who could handle the technical side of things.

At this point thing began to get confused.

I found myself shouting in frustration through a Skype connection at my client in Beijing. I believe that, technically, this is something you are not supposed to do when someone is gracious enough to employ you. To be fair, it was a two-way street. Xi Li shouted at me too.

I can't remember which of us was the first to do so.

Show One in the lineup (of four) was a pop concert.

Over and above the lighting specifications, which were colossal, there was smoke, there were pyrotechnics, various flying pieces, various trucking pieces, bespoke set pieces and of course the inevitable LED screen. There was talk of installing a whole floor on top of the stage with tracks, so that two grand pianos could be winched on and off. Minute discussions began between the Hong Kong team and our UK production manager. Virtually every piece of backstage equipment in Europe was being requisitioned for the Olympics, so these exquisitely detailed emails consumed precious time,

At the same time as I met Zhou Kim, the Beijing team planning Show Three—the orchestral concert—sent a lady designer to London. Back in Beijing she had asked me about the cost of manufacturing some giant drapes that she wanted to hang in the Hoxton Empire. I told her that I would get three quotes. When we met again in London, she asked me "When do we see the factories?"

I had said, "quotes," but she had understood, "factories." She was dismayed that there were no factories for her to visit. I was amazed at the mistranslation that had occurred. She was concerned to the point of trauma, which made me fear for what she might be facing on her return to Beijing. I made some swift calls and arranged a visit to a factory in North London, which manufactured stage fabrics, for the following morning. We found solutions. The lady designer went home, happy.

The Hong Kong team fielded ever-more detailed and frequent emails, but the Beijing team, their lady designer having returned to them, fell silent. I suggested to Zhou Kim, to Molly, and to Xi Li that conference calls with the various teams would be a good idea. Instead, Xi Li directed me to pass all communication through Zhou Kim, who seemed to speak and understand less English as each day passed, and it became clear that zero information went beyond this guy in either direction. Somewhere behind the scenes there were people making the decisions about the budget.

When problems came up, and there was no response to my questions, it was as if a careful intermediary was whispering into my ear, "The Emperor is not in the mood to hear bad news today."

I set up a meeting with the orchestra management in London. Margaret, Lucy, Ben, and Steve on the management side were there, along with Zhou Kim, Molly and me. Steve, an efficient and genial man, addressed the issues.

"I wonder if it would be possible to have the music in Western musical notation?"

"Yes, I understand." said Zhou Kim.

"If we could get that as soon as possible, it would be very helpful," said Steve, "and the guest artists...would it be possible to know who they are?"

"Yes," said Zhou Kim, "I understand."

"And could we get confirmation that the video recording fee has been agreed?"

Molly translated.

"Shenme!?" said Zhou Kim.

"What!?" said Molly—translating.

I pitched in. "If the concert is to be filmed, a fee will have to be paid. We've talked about this before."

"Ah," said Zhou Kim, "Yes, I understand."

And I really think he did.

A long flight later I was back in Beijing for one sweltering week. By now, it was full summer and really hot. All praise to the Beijing tree-planting policy. Along the above-ground subway rides in the north of the city I saw teams of workers planting trees. And the trees on the boulevards were growing well, appreciably more robust than when I saw them first in 2008, and staving off at least ten degrees of heat with their shade. This planting mitigated the worst of the spring dust storms. The Gobi Desert, where the dust comes from, still advances by hundreds of miles each year, despite the efforts of Beijing's green wall.

I did not see Xi Li in Beijing during the humid week—no matter that it was one of the reasons I had made this extra around-the-world trip.

I imagine that Xi Li would have liked to replace me. She couldn't, the venue wouldn't have let the project go forward. I would like to have quit, but instead, and for reasons that even now I find hard to understand, I decided it was a once in a lifetime chance to deploy the kind of impossibly high standards of compassion and ethical conduct exhibited by more advanced practitioners of Buddhism. Viz: I would try to maintain an attitude of encouragement no matter what, adorn the situation with positive thinking, and generally try to be hospitable to the guests in our country.

Does that all sound a bit inflated? It does to me, so, don't worry—I'm able to tell you that as a deeply flawed human being I didn't quite make it.

Sadly, because of a mix of contradictory expectations and a tangle of multi-party obligations, my relationship with Xi Li had been declining to a point beyond salvage. There had been a loss of face all round. This is something people go to huge lengths to avoid in China, but I couldn't worry about it. There wasn't time.

It was no surprise when the next installment of my fee did not arrive. A week past the due date I sent an email to Xi Li with a subject line that said, "Please read this carefully." I explained that if she did not pay me, I would not be able to pay my team, and the project would collapse. To be fair, it must have been as frustrating for her as for me. I have no way of knowing.

But I got paid. It was bitter wages.

I went back to London, where I stayed with Mike and learned something important.

Mike was an old friend from drama school, a northern lad who became fascinated with Spain and all things Spanish. Odd that, but then you never know with foreign countries, do you? Spain for him; China for me. Mike is a splendid actor. Detailed and meticulous.

Do you have a bag full of plastic shopping bags somewhere? And do you, like me, forget to take the ecologically correct, reusable bag when you nip out to the supermarket for milk? Which means that you come back with yet another plastic bag? This is where Mike comes in. He demonstrated with a bag, uttering the words, "Watch carefully—you'll thank me later."

He smoothed the bag carefully on a flat surface, removing the air and taking out any creases. Then he folded it along its length to make a strip two inches wide. Then starting at the bottom, he folded the left corner over to make an equilateral triangle—like they fold flags at solemn ceremonies. He repeated the triangular folding all along the length of the bag, leaving a final tail that he tucked neatly into the previous triangle. He had reduced a sprawling plastic confusion to a manageable geometric shape that could be stacked next to several dozen others. A masterpiece of space-saving. This can be done with complete safety in the comfort of your own home, taking marginally less time out of your day than it would to iron a shirt.

As I said, meticulous and painstaking. To this day Mike remains a superb actor. He takes great care and time with his work. He has a book on his shelves with the unlikely title, *Spanish in Three Months*—my underline. Beyond the life-changing technique which makes compact plastic samosas out of shopping bags, I was also grateful for his generous hospitality.

Production week was approaching. The shows could not go on sale until the contract was signed—the nth in a series that had attempted to keep up with all the changes of program. This couldn't happen until we knew we could confirm the orders, which couldn't happen till Xi Li had the money from her sub-letters and Chen Ling collated all the bureaucratic requirements, and transferred the money to London. And none of that would happen until the budgets were approved. Each day the UK team tried to move forward to an agreement, but none of us knew what information got passed to the Chinese side.

There was spectacular confusion around ticket sales.

Demands would be issued that high-level dignitaries in London attend the shows and be given canapés and wine. I would get prices for space and catering, then the idea would be cancelled. Or it would be decided that tickets should be given away to fill the theater, and the next day that a commission-based sales team should be pounding the phones.

Molly, my interpreter, tried to explain things to me. The Chinese approach to what is possible involves exhaustive discussion and exploration, and final decisions are made only when every possible aspect has been examined. Unfortunately she had already booked another gig and I couldn't persuade her to stay on through the coming productions. If she had not been there I think I would have considered taking a one-way flight to Fiji, and staying there until the Olympics—and these shows—were over and forgotten.

One night I woke up in a pool of sweat, shaking with nerves. Why? Because I had too much responsibility and not enough control. A perfect formula for stress. Why should I have cared? I cared because I had given commitments to people in both countries, and now several dozen professionals in the United Kingdom were involved. I also wanted the shows to work. I thought in some small way it would further the cause of world peace—though less so as each day passed.

For remedy I visited the place on Earth that I think is nearest to paradise—Hampstead Heath. The heath is seven hundred acres of well-managed semi-wild woods, meadows, and ponds in north London. It has a uniquely English feel to it, reflected in all seasons. This was summer, and the grasses were waist high, and once up the southern side of Parliament Hill I looked to wooded slopes, where the light shifted and gently shimmered as I meandered toward one of the Hampstead pubs.

A quart of cleansing ale, and I felt a lot better about it all.

Deadlines with suppliers came and went. It was the Olympics, in case anyone had forgotten. Suppliers were persuaded to keep our orders open on condition of 100 percent payment upfront. It was clear that my Chinese colleagues thought that I was profiting hugely from the situation.

The precise opposite was the case. I had, in the heat of argument, given up my profit in the project to engage Selena Smith at my own expense. In hindsight I see it was folly to hope this would create some warm fuzzy feelings and cement a basis for future business.

It got worse.

Somewhere in all the confusion Selena placed an order for two set pieces from a bespoke model maker. The pieces were a three-dimensional whale and a large bird's wing, custom-made to high specification, fire proofed (as per UK regulations) and costing about £10,000. I was not aware for three days that the order had been placed, by which time it was too late to cancel it. The Hong Kong design team at first refused to confirm the order, then they said they didn't want it. I took responsibility for this snafu and laid out the money personally. I had no idea whether I would be able to recover this money, nor whether the pieces would be used in the show.

A more seasoned producer would not have allowed himself to become personally liable in this way, and it embarrasses me to admit to such a mistake. But hey! If it all went horribly, horribly wrong, I would have a ten-foot whale and an equally large bird's wing with beautifully painted feathers, to do with whatever I wished. Surely no living room, or garden, should be without such decorative accessories. For covering this disaster I received bare acknowledgement and no thanks.

It was deeply fortunate the design team now went into change-your-mind mode. As soon as the decision about the whale and the wing tipped in my favor, I confirmed the order in writing with all parties. Getting reimbursed was akin to drawing teeth from the proverbial dragon, but I managed it eventually.

In the midst of too much detail from the Hong Kong team and none at all from the Beijing team, somehow at last the budgets were agreed upon. Here, I think, there was direct intervention from the Goddess Kwan Yin. By now there were three weeks before production week, and all suppliers had gone beyond all agreed deadlines. This would have been a crisis situation at the best of times, let alone now—the Olympics, remember?

I Skyped the formidable comptroller Chen Ling, "How soon can you get the money here?"

"You always worry about the money!"

"Well, you see...er...oh...never mind. When?"

"Friday."

All London suppliers were contacted and once again sweet-talked to holding everything until Friday.

I went for a walk. London is the city of my birth, and I spent most of my childhood and youth there. I'd been away for some years. It was a pleasant English summer, and the city, spurred by the Olympics, was looking good.

The place had undergone some design initiatives. The available coffee was now as good as that in Sydney—which I reckon leads the world in the arts and sciences of coffee making. The infrastructure had been overhauled. The north London overground, which takes in Hampstead Heath and rolls around the west of the city to the other great park at Richmond, is a specially pleasant journey. And although London fares will never be able to compete with the Beijing flat rate of 2 kuai, the Tube is ever improving.

The production budget was on the way, at least the shows would get on. I was sorry that, with the best will in the world, I had lost the confidence of certain people on the Chinese side. My business acumen had advanced by one expensive lesson—it almost never works to try to do favors for people who don't trust you. But at least I had facilitated the project and it would happen. Because the money was on the way.

Friday came. No money.

"Colin," said Selena, normally an example of grace under pressure, "what's going on?" Had she been talking to Rosie? The phrase sounded familiar.

So began yet another telephone, Skype, text and email exchange at Olympic level.

"What do you want me to tell my suppliers?" asked Selena.

"Tell them..." I took a few minutes to think about this. I was in no mood to incur more financial loss, which is what asking the suppliers to keep their orders open could have led to if the production money never came. I could have said, "Tell them it's over, let them to take their kit and their people to the other events clamoring for their stuff." But If I had said that, what would have been the fallout if, as, and when the money did in fact come in? And, I thought to myself, my client and colleagues were now considerably invested in the event, weren't they? Travel had been booked, accommodation and all the rest of it...which meant that surely the money would come...didn't it?

I took a couple of breaths, "Selena, tell them to keep the orders open."

"Till when?"

"Well it's the weekend, nothing will get here till Monday. Can you persuade them to hold everything till then?"

"I don't know."

The dough did not arrive over the weekend, all banks being closed. Nor on the Monday.

I wonder if I can convey the state of nerves this created in the London team? That Monday was the day when it really seemed as if the whole project might collapse. I kept checking with our book-keeper at two hourly intervals.

I took another walk on Hampstead Heath. This time it did not help.

Selena called. "I have managed to keep everyone on board for one more day. But if the money isn't there tomorrow. That's it. It's over."

"Okay." It was the only thing to say.

My mind turned to great commercial disasters in history. Knowing that no amount of cleansing ale would assuage my anxiety and that I probably wouldn't sleep that night, I went to play poker at one of the twenty-four hour card rooms in Leicester Square. The level of play had improved greatly since my last time in London. Poker is a deep game and Texas Hold'em is a deep variation. I won £100. Well, if I should find myself facing multiple six figure liability in the morning, it was a start. Where, I wondered, would I find that kind of money? Not as an actor, that's for sure.

On Tuesday morning, at the absolute last possible moment—all the UK suppliers were on the verge of canceling orders for equipment and technicians—the money arrived in our bookkeeper's account. I requested an instant transfer, and orders were confirmed. There were now seventeen days before the equipment was due to be installed in the theater. "Pushing it for time" doesn't come close to describing the pressure and the financial risk.

Steve, from the orchestral management, called. "I know you've got a lot on your plate," he began, "How's everything going by the way?"

"Fine," I said, "couldn't be better."

"Good," said Steve, "because over here we're all wondering wtf is going on?"

Where had I heard words like that before?

"I suppose," I said, falling in with the welcome irony, "that this would be because you don't have the music, and therefore don't know the orchestration, which means that you can't make final bookings of the musicians, you don't know if transcription services will be required, you have no idea who the guest artists are, have not finalized the rehearsal schedule, and don't know where the guest Chinese musicians fit in."

"Yes," Steve said, "all of that."

"Anything else?"

We covered one or two more items, each requiring urgent attention, and I said I would get back to him asap.

I called Zhou Kim.

The man was charm itself. Truly, I warmed to him whenever we spoke. He did have a beatific smile, and even though we were on the phone I could imagine it easily, having seen it a thousand times when he uttered his usual one-liner.

I should also pay respect to his patience. For the past several weeks I had frequently pressed him for information, and far from telling me, "These ceaseless demands have to stop!", he was a model of courtesy. This time was no exception. "Yes," he told me, as I went through each pressing issue, "I understand."

I called Steve again and he took me through the possible scenario if certain things were not resolved. Among the images he conjured was that of a sixty-five piece orchestra—one of the finest in Europe—sitting there with their instruments, in full evening dress, but not making any sounds. That is, not playing any music.

"Let's talk again soon." I said, wondering if I was still eligible for NHS services and could get some prescription tranquilizers.

The shows could now be officially put on sale. With two and a half weeks to go, in Olympic season, the prospects for a large audience were not good. And swaths of London were strangely empty. Businesses everywhere were complaining about lack of trade. It was the Olympics of course. Everybody wanted to watch the Games, and they all flocked to the Olympic stadium which held about eighty thousand. Meanwhile, the Hoxton Empire, which held about one thousand, was looking pretty empty.

Zhou Kim called me.

"I am Zhou Kim."

"I know."

"We want the theater to be full."

"Yes. Me too."

"We are not selling any tickets."

"I know."

"Why not?"

I took a couple of breaths, and debated whether it was worth going through the list. Of course it wasn't. Even though Zhou Kim's English was coming along in—well not exactly leaps and bounds—let's say bite-sized nuggets, it would have been tough at this point to get the man to grasp the implications of things that had already been explained a dozen ways on a daily basis for several months.

"Zhou Kim," I said, speaking slowly, "with less than three weeks to go, there is only one way to fill the theater."

I sensed impatience at the other end. "If we ever do this again," Zhou Kim said, speaking equally slowly and carefully, "we will find a British producer who understands marketing."

I thought through a couple of possible responses. There was some ripe stuff from the Shakespearean canon I could have unleashed—but I knew this man was not my audience for those pentameters. The truth is, I was frustrated because of my lack of Mandarin vocabulary. Finally I said what I should have been saying all along, *"Shi de. Wo ming bai."*

Which means, "Yes, I understand."

We came to production week and Show One.

A crowd of media types rolled into town, including one super-slim, glamorous chick who laid down the law about audience attendance. Leave aside the facts for a moment. Like it didn't go on sale till less than three weeks ago, like there'd been no publicity because…oh, never mind…actually, yes, let's mind.

The London publicist retained by the theater who would have been able to deliver excellent coverage, had been asking for materials for months. Nothing had been supplied. By going to some considerable trouble, with three days till show time, she arranged a press conference with the main London evening newspaper. There could not have been better publicity. Had the Chinese contingent and their star attended, as they had agreed to do, I would guestimate that sales would have quintupled. The morning of the press event came and went. The pop star and her entourage did not turn up. No explanation was given.

"Colin," said Rosie the next day. "What the fuck's going on?"

I couldn't have put it better myself.

I suppose I could have mentioned all this to Superslim, but it's unlikely she would have heard a word, because listening did not appear to be in her skill set, and what good would it have done anyway?

Meanwhile, the marketing manager at Hoxton Empire asked me to prepare a spreadsheet of who had requisitioned what tickets, whether attendance had been confirmed, and so on.

I duly prepared the spreadsheet and asked Superslim to tell me how many tickets she had put around town. She began to shrilly question me. "Why? Why do you need this information?" Before I could answer, she yelled again, "Why!?"

This outburst had a charm all of its own, as we were very publicly seated in the theater coffee bar. Luckily one of my interpreters was there, and they had a long, heated discussion that will never be translated. Finally Superslim screamed in English, "If I paid for it, I can do it the way I want!"

There was a third set piece. A large egg, from which the young pop star would emerge at the beginning of the show.

To construct this piece, in accordance with fireproofing regulations—using fiberglass—was an expensive undertaking requiring specialist knowledge. The quote from quality model makers was unacceptable to our Chinese colleagues.

The Egg was cut from the specifications, then reinstated, then cut again.

Zhou Kim, as I've said before, was a thoroughly winning personality. Here's a small example of his brilliance. There had been at least six changes of mind about the Egg within the past week. Then Zhou Kim sourced someone via the Internet. His Internet search was based upon the word "model"—evidently he was looking for a "model maker." Instead he turned up a "glamour model photographer," the kind that takes photographs of people with not too many clothes on. This person said, "Sure, I'll make you an Egg!" I expect he also asked if Zhou Kim would like a fur-lined one, and maybe a bridge and some blue sky to go with it.

Selena made a further online search and discovered that the "glamour model photographer" had litigation for fraudulent practices pending. It was my duty to communicate these facts to my client, Xi Li, which I did, giving the information without prejudice. The Egg was promptly dropped.

Then, with two days to go until the show, it was announced that the Egg was back, supplied by yet another artisan. I emailed Chen Ling, the comptroller in Beijing, to confirm this, as there were financial implications. Her swift response was completely clear:

"There is no Egg. Please don't talk about it any more."

Well, at least we knew where we stood in regard to the Egg. It wasn't happening.

The Egg arrived late at night during the last technical rehearsal.

It was made of cut-price found materials and covered in pond liner. Clearly, it was not fireproof. All the next day a swarm of unknown people worked on this set piece on the pavement behind the theater, covering it in plaster and paint. Wrangling negotiations among Selena, Griff the user-friendly resident technical director, the designers from China, and Chinese artisans from London, continued during any spare moments. I stayed out of it.

I suggested to Superslim, via Zhou Kim, that if they followed the box-office manager's advice about ticket allocation, the theater would fill up in an orderly, logical fashion. This suggestion was discounted as evidence of Western Imperialism, and consequently the day before the show the box-office chart of the audience looked like the head of a man with badly thinning hair.

In the middle of the day—this was Wednesday, and the pop concert was having its final dress-rehearsal—Hugh Wong arrived. He was wrangling the musical director of the orchestral concert—Saturday's show. I wondered who Mr. Wong was, but the two of them agreed to pay the disputed recording fee. "That's great," I said. "Because tomorrow is the absolute final deadline."

This followed a collector's item of a phone conversation between Zhou Kim and me the previous night.

"We will just use this recording for archive purposes. We will be very responsible about this," he said.

"Zhou Kim," I said. "Do you seriously think that with an eight-camera, hi-def, broadcast-quality shoot in place, and one hundred and twenty-eight channels of the finest sound equipment available, anyone will believe you're just going to show this to a few friends at the Spring Festival?"

He hung up.

Hugh Wong took me aside. "Surely you can arrange a special price."

I tried to explain that the Musicians' Union is one of the most powerful in Europe, and goes to great lengths to make sure its members are protected and compensated for their services. These attempts at explanation just—what's the word?—missed. Have you ever told a joke that no one laughed at? It was a bit like that.

To be fair, all Chinese players in the mix were baffled as to why a recording fee had to be paid. In China you video whatever you want, unless the government tells you not to. You wouldn't think of paying for it.

Also, to be fair, I became aware that my client, Xi Li, was facing pressures of her own back in Beijing. We'd had conversations that made it clear she was as anxious as I was, for different reasons. As I said before, I admired her theatrical entrepreneurship. No question but that I had lost my cool more than once during this process, but I felt for her, as I sensed tensions beyond my comprehension.

That night London's Chinese community came out in force for Show One and began to patchily fill the theater. No one knew which tickets had been confirmed—my careful spreadsheet lay on a desk somewhere, ornamenting a vacant office—and the box office was ten feet deep in the sounds of many dialects. Because of this the show began almost forty minutes late, and had me praying that we did not run into overtime. The Egg was there in the opening tableau. How it got there was at the top of my list of Things I Do Not Want to Know. After all, I was only the producer.

The stalls were about sixty percent full, with the aforementioned balding effect all over. All during the performance Superslim ferried people from the upper circle down three flights of stairs and placed them in the stalls. I caught her eye at one point, and she looked at me with undisguised triumph and contempt. I gave her a slight nod of approval, and I was happy to let her have it. After all, she was paying for it.

The media were there in force. A six-camera shoot, this was separate from the shoot for Show Three, had been requested, arranged, and yes, paid for—a day or two beyond the last minute of course. China TV called—at the last minute—and requested access, which they got.

About a gazillion people with cameras on tripods were also there, none of whom we had been told about, none of whom had security passes, none of whom…oh, never mind. Anyway, they were all there. And the media were pointing their cameras at the joyous, transported, delighted faces of the audience—for retailing purposes back in the People's Republic of China.

Superslim had also shrilled at me, "but we need Western faces, Western!" She and her staff—all factions of the visiting production team had lots of staff—continued to ferry people from the upper circle to the stalls, so that by the end of the concert, when the moment of official, happy, egalitarian harmony between our two nations had arrived, all manner of confetti and streamers were fired from cannons out into the audience, and the cameras were turned away from the stage and onto the auditorium to record the joy. By now, the stalls were actually packed. Not a single empty seat.

I had personally supplied some six or so Western faces, friends, whom minions in the PR entourage had placed well off to the side in the dress circle, pretty much out of shot. But I am sure there must have been some Western faces somewhere. Hamish, the rock-n-roll guy who supplied twenty singing kids at the last minute? Er, no, he was standing at the back with me, exclaiming, "It doesn't get better than this!" Rosie, the chief executive? No, she had left early because they'd been told to close the bars, and she was a little peeved about lost revenue—so not her. But I'm sure there were some somewhere.

There was a Western face on stage. A guest pop artist had come on, but with the special virtue—in a pop concert—that he could actually sing. He really stood out for his two numbers, one of which had obliquely anodyne political lyrics: "You don't get what's happening/you want to/but you can't..." He used his winning personality to invite the audience to join in the chorus, which they politely declined to do—maybe because English was foreign to them.

Show Two, the next day, was a children's talent show. I had been told to expect one hundred teenagers from twelve to sixteen years of age. Accordingly, on the morning of the show we took delivery of one hundred and twenty infants from five to ten years of age. The requisite number of chaperones escorted them. The show was quite lovely, the kids performed some charming songs and dances, there was some excellent calligraphy and some entertaining puppetry. The performance put a glow of feel-good over the whole theater.

One odd thing happened. At forty-five minutes to curtain the kids were all sitting in the dress circle, from where they would be accompanied to the stage and back, and a Kentucky Fried Chicken dinner was distributed to each of them—Colonel Sanders, it seems, is first cousin to General Tso. There are regulations about eating front of house in England. I told myself—"Relax!" You can overdo the rules sometimes. Edward, the stage manager, appeared with black plastic bags and as the audience came in we filled them.

And then there was Friday, when preparations began for Show Three.

At 9:00 a.m. I called Selena. She was a highly competent professional who had saved the project from the chaos that would unquestionably have ensued had she not been there. She was expertly assisted by her colleague Edward Green, who acted as company stage manager.

"Hi Selena, I'm going to be little late. Got some errands to run, okay with you?"

"No problem."

And I was confident that she was correct, and could handle anything that came up. Our relations had become slightly frayed—in my opinion, given the circs, it was miraculous that we were still speaking. A situation had arisen when—how shall I put this?—everything that was going on meant that I only managed to get the vital insurances (without which I could not have allowed any of the several hundred Chinese visitors access to the theater) in place at about 4:00 p.m. on the Friday afternoon before the Sunday morning get-in. Last minute? Er, kind of.

"What am I going to do," I had asked, just slightly frantic, "if I don't get the certificates? Take them all to the local Chinese restaurant for lunch?!"

There was a pause. I heard Selena taking a few deep breaths at the other end of the line. Finally she said, "Good idea!"

You may gather this was a conversation alive with subtext.

Anyway, it was now exactly one week later, and *this* Friday I told her I would be late. The only errand that mattered was to see if the vital video-recording fee had been paid.

I had had a difficult phone call with the comptroller, Chen Ling, the previous midnight, when I insisted the money must be in London on this day. She left me thinking she wasn't sure if it would be. With China being seven hours ahead of UK time, this meant that banks were already closed there, and with this being Friday, if she had not put a rush on it, and it didn't arrive till Monday, it would be too late! This Friday morning was, of course, one day past the absolute deadline, and the last possible business day that the funds could be transferred. If the money didn't come today, and there were cameras in the theater tomorrow, the orchestra would sit there, but they would not play.

Everybody in the mix knew this—Xi Li, Chen Ling, Xiao Xue, Zhou Kim, Hugh Wong, various assistants and Long Shun. They knew it, because I had told them, the orchestral management had told them, the venue had told them and I told them all again. But did they really know it? I could not be sure.

I set out from Walthamstow for the West End. For some unexplained reason, there were no Victoria Line trains to Central London. I just got the last train going south, which took me one stop to Tottenham Hale. I grabbed a taxi. The twenty-five-minute tube journey became a forty-five-minute £100 cab ride. By 11:00 a.m. we had only made it to Regent's Park. I stopped the cab when I could no longer stand seeing the pounds evaporating, and I walked briskly down through Covent Garden. My phone went. It was Steve from orchestra management.

"Has it come yet."

"Terrible line," I said, and hung up.

This was a morning when the sun had risen on the ashes of a singular conversation the previous day. The disputed fee had been agreed upon. But it only related to the actual performance. So it was a surprise when a camera crew had turned up in the rehearsal hall, unannounced, not negotiated, unpaid for, completely surplus to anything agreed upon in the contract. They had started to film the rehearsal, were stopped, started again, were stopped and asked to leave.

The formidable Chen Ling called Steve. "This is fucking bullshit," she said.

Steve stated that be that as it may, the contractual situation was clear.

"When the BBC Symphony comes to China," fumed Chen Ling, "I will make it very difficult for them."

"When the BBC Symphony comes to China," returned Steve—tactfully not mentioning that not one person in any way connected with any of these shows was actually working for the BBC—"you are perfectly at liberty to do as you wish. But at the moment you are dealing with the UK, so you'll have to do things the UK way."

Chen Ling ended the conversation without saying "Goodbye."

I reached the heart of the West End and climbed the stairs to the swank office of one of the most successful producing organizations of the late twentieth century. I asked the man providing accounting services for us if the expected money had turned up.

It had not.

I left the office. Time seemed to have run out. I didn't know if the tube was back on line, in any case I needed to walk to clear my head and think. As I went up the Charing Cross Road, I got a text. "Presenter must attend tonight's rehearsal." Unsigned. Who was it from? Ah, Hugh Wong.

As per my brief I had also engaged a presenter. There had been several changes of mind about whether she was needed for the evening's rehearsal or not. The phone went. It was Hugh Wong. "This is incredibly important," he said.

He sounded jumpy. It was as if he faced a terrible consequence.

"The rehearsal is in three hours time. You want the presenter there?" I asked.

"Yes, that's right."

"You cancelled that to save money."

"Yes, I know, but we want her to come. It's very important."

"Ok, I'll see what I can do. There will be a fee."

I continued walking north up the Tottenham Court Road, and called the presenter's agent. Could Ms. Hatter now come to the Friday evening rehearsal? The agent said she'd see what she could do.

I continued walking, wracking my brains for a solution to the expensive nightmare brewing over at the theater. The only thing I could think of was to broker an on-the-spot agreement among the several parties as to how the filming could possibly proceed—this, let's face it, being the main reason for this group's presence in London. I would suggest withholding the recorded material until the money was cleared in the orchestra's bank account. Would anybody agree to that? It seemed unlikely. I had a plan, not much of one, but I was ready to face the tube.

The phone rang. It was Zhou Kim. "We don't want the female presenter to come."

"But Hugh Wong just called me to say you did want her."

"I know," said Zhou Kim. "But, er, now, we don't want."

I called the agent back. "They don't want her to come."

"They don't?"

"No."

I made the necessary apologies and entered Warren Street Underground.

I said before that the London Tube is constantly improving, and it is. But London transportation doesn't come cheap. Two tube lines and an overground train later, the pounds on my oyster card having taken a further bashing, I arrived at the theater to find the set in place, as agreed upon, but looking pretty scrappy—the special drapes had not yet been dressed.

All the orchestra members had their musical-instrument cases sitting between their chairs.

Everyone was hot. The lighting crew was playing with the lights, which was making it difficult for the musicians to rehearse, the visiting Chinese Maestro was getting testy. Long Shun, the visiting Chinese director, was nipping at the heels of the British camera crew. The translators were earning their money. The stage was crowded, tempers were short.

My phone went. It was our book-keeper. "The money just came in. As per your instructions I paid by instant transfer—cost you another fifteen quid."

It was 4:00 p.m., exactly one hour before the close of business on a Friday afternoon. Money which should have been in place weeks ago had finally arrived. "Thank you." I said.

There's a wonderful story about the late, great British actress, Beryl Reid. One day a keen young director gave her some detailed notes. She stopped him, saying "Darling, you are confusing me with someone who gives a fuck!"

Even though the sentiments expressed by the incomparable Ms. Reid exactly described my own view by this point in the proceedings, the relief that the money had come was huge. I suppose it had something to do with the fact that a project I had been connected with for almost a year was not going to collapse in a slew of acrimony, accusation and embarrassment..

At that moment, Xiao Xue, the astonishingly beautiful star of Show Three, appeared in the first of a series of extraordinary frocks. From where I was at the back of the orchestra stalls she glowed with the enigmatic light of the mysterious Orient. There was a jet-black frock sparkling with diamante, and then a red one with silk tresses and trains. She knew how to wear this gear and she was damn easy to look at. The very air around her seemed numinous. This transcendent perception lasted only briefly. The choir (forty-five of them), the orchestra (sixty-seven of them), and a grand piano were there, alongside the star. The lights were changing colors and going up and down as the technicians tried to build cues. The Chinese Maestro conducting finally lost his cool.

"Who," he thundered, "is in charge of the lighting!"

I was back in the real world.

The technicians realized they would have to fix the cues in the small hours after rehearsal and the stage was returned to a general wash of light.

I had engaged another two bilingual ladies, Lily and Carol, to interpret for me. I collected one of them and approached Long Shun—he's a big deal back in the Middle Kingdom. I apologized for not being there during the day, and explained that I had had some "administrative tasks" to attend to. I said nothing regarding the hair's breadth between the arrival of the money and a possible international incident. He had previously darted me a dark look, which I think might have had to do with my absence. But now he smiled, and we talked about solving the spacing problems.

We went outside so that we wouldn't disturb the number being rehearsed. Long Shun immediately lit a cigarette. Selena appeared as though from a tele-porter and offered solutions, also lighting up. Long Shun liked it that she smoked. Smoking is a very popular activity in China. It was a moment of rapport. I was glad. I warmed to the man. His entire retinue treated him with a level of deference that one imagines is a hangover from Imperial times, and he did have extraordinary charm and charisma. The rehearsal ended with a production meeting where Long Shun went through the issues one by one without notes—he was a pro. Selena noted each one down, although of course she was already aware of all of them—she was a pro.

The Saturday performance the following night worked like clockwork. Long Shun had conferred with his British counterpart, the director of the camera crew, and without interpreters, but through hand signals, they had made each other understand the kind of shots they wanted. It was excellent to see two professionals so steeped in their craft that they could understand each other very well without speech. Both men smiled, as did I. In that moment I witnessed the best communication of the entire year-long project.

Selena was efficiency itself and supplied Long Shun with a score-reader and shot-caller. He also had Lily, one of the best interpreters in Britain, stationed at his side throughout the show. The show itself was received rapturously. The set design was truly spectacular, and the famous drapes, now dressed and lit as the lady designer had wanted, showed off the theater very well.

The star, Xiao Xue, was——well, a star! As well as her radiant beauty, she had a voice that reached to the back of the Upper Circle, and the audience loved her.

At the end of the show, as the audience was leaving, Hugh Wong happened to remark, "Oh, I spoke to Chen Ling and she told me she already sent the money for the recording fee - the day before yesterday."

I gaped at the man. This meant that when we spoke on the phone she had known that the money would arrive in time. At the very last minute, but in time. She knew, and she didn't tell me. So that whole morning. The taxi. The strategizing. The nervous energy...oh, never mind. We got through Show Three.

One more to go, and then it would all be over.

I went backstage and climbed up to the company office on the fifth floor.

This theatrical collection of four shows from China had been marketed as feel-good Olympic exchange. Some of the material had flirted close to copyright infringement. So much so, that wishing to protect my client, I had checked things out with the legal office at the Olympic village and had spoken with a charming lawyer.

"Well, these performances are only one-night stands," he said. "If all you're doing is saying how nice it was that the last Olympics were in Beijing, and how nice it is now that they're in London…"

"That's right." I said. "Feel-good factor between our two nations."

"No problem!" he said. "I mean, it's not as if you're using any copyrighted images, is it?"

"Oh no!" I said.

So that was fine.

When I got to the office, I saw that four large cardboard boxes full of programs for the next day's show had been delivered. I took a program and looked at it. It was covered in the Olympic logo. In unofficial colors. I thought about immediately calling the Lord Mayor of London to appeal for flexibility, but it was now 2:00 a.m.

Downstairs the set from the orchestral concert had been pulled apart in preparation for the new fit-up for the Sunday show. At that moment there was nothing I could do. I went home, if not to sleep, then to count—not sheep—but at least the colored beads of a mental abacus.

In the morning I returned to the theater early. I just wanted to get through the day without incident.

As I walked through the stage door, one of the Peking Opera performers was being rushed to the emergency room. Selena was in full-out management mode and fortunately both our splendid interpreters were on hand. One of them, Carol, accompanied the casualty to the hospital. The diagnosis came back a few hours later. A sudden flare-up of herpes had given the unlucky young man swellings all over his face—even Peking

Opera make-up would not hide them. It meant that he had to be quarantined from the rest of the company. The company was carrying no medical insurance. I am proud to say that at the hospital he was treated free of charge.

The show was re-worked to accommodate the loss of one of the leading players, and the matinee went up on time. I had placed a special conference call to China the previous week, with Lily interpreting for me, to check out some of the activities in the show. I had been told there would be plenty of Gong Fu, but not full contact.

"Any weapons?" I had asked the director. "Any tumbling?"

"No, no, just Gong Fu."

The show was indeed chock-full of Gong Fu. There were also plenty of both weapons and tumbling. It was spectacular. Great to watch. Thrilling!

Unless you happened to be the London producer standing at the back of the orchestra stalls, aware that we were not insured for these particular activities, and thinking about unlimited employers' liability, or unlimited public liability, should some mishap carry beyond the footlights.

It was a fitting peak of personal anxiety that somehow seemed both appropriate to the year-long behind-the-scenes drama, and also inevitable. I deployed various internal techniques to calm myself. I took deep martial-arts style breaths, I counted backwards and forwards to one hundred in Chinese, I asked myself how one of the re-incarnated Buddhas of Compassion would have coped. This Peking Opera performance was a compact ninety-five minutes, but I came close to understanding the nature of eternity as I watched.

It was a nervous conclusion to a year's involvement with a project that had morphed into strange forms.

And the programs? It is fair to say that there is a different view of copyright in China. Somehow—I've no idea how it could have happened—the programs had got themselves locked in a cupboard, the key to the cupboard could not be found, and the programs were not distributed.

Perhaps it was for the best.

Political!?

This book is an anecdotal memoir. But here I pause and ask myself what it all meant.

The first thought that surfaces is that maybe I should write this chapter under a pseudonym—the little known Celtic author Lachloin McNilpy, perhaps? Or the undiscovered novelist Chilmlay Plomcin?

Going back to the lady behind the glass at the consulate, with her mildly hostile tone...so what if I was a political writer? Which I'm not. I'd just like to make that clear. But so what if I was? Would it be so terrible if I put some words down about...oh, I don't know...pollution, the ruling plutocracy, and human rights abuses that disgrace the species? Just suppose I wrote anything on any of these topics. Would it alter (fill in the blank for nationality) government policy by the tiniest fraction of a hair's breadth of one scruple?

This free speech business...

Watch the overstimulated TV anchor people of US cable news, and you've got to admit they talk loudly. Even if you turn the volume down to just barely audible they still seem to be shouting. This is where the Chinese approach to control of the public mind has greater effectiveness. Well, at least it's quieter. Watch the English-language State TV in Beijing, and the feature of the anchor people is that there is no ranting, and no raving. Instead there is polite discussion in impeccable English. It was persuasive.

I grew up in England and also went to school for a while in Australia. Now I live in America. As a young man I decided that as long as my government left me alone I would return the favor. When I was about fourteen I went to see a debate in the House of Commons. It wasn't until I had lived another fourteen years that I could bring myself to vote. I was appalled. To the extent that I took a famous bit of London graffiti to be the summit of political wisdom - *Don't Vote, it Only Encourages Them.* A complacent stance, uninformed and primitive, and I did move on from it. I read Plato's *The Republic.*

In China some forms are similar to Western ones, some not. In Australia universal suffrage is supported in law, as a citizen you are required to vote. In China not so much. In the spring in Beijing there's a lot of cherry blossom. It's beautiful. The same way that cherry blossom in London is beautiful, and in Washington D. C. It's illegal to play poker and gamble in mainland China. It's illegal to play poker online in the United States. The Chinese Las Vegas equivalent is off-shore in Macau, where you can gamble as much as you like. Outlawing gambling in China is about as realistic as outlawing pasta in Italy.

During my time in Beijing I had come across a discreet poker game on Saturday nights. It took place in a certain part of town not far from the local police station. In a bar where they sold a watered-down beer so incredibly cheaply that no one minded its taste and the ferocious headache it gave you the following morning. The game was one thousand yuan ($130) to enter, and the last three standing split the money. The players were mostly ex-patriate English teachers, a group of desperadoes such as you might find in some frontier town. It wasn't an oil rig we were working on, but there in the bar, it felt like one. The characters wore flamboyant hats and told fabulous tales of multiple five-figure monthly earnings to each other, claiming to be in business consultancy. They even seemed to believe it themselves.

An important Chinese word is *guanxi*. It means "relationship", and a whole lot more. Someone who is well connected is said to have good *guanxi*. The equivalent of the Western "knowing the right people." Nothing happens in China without *guanxi*. People with better qualifications are passed over in favor of nephews and nieces. Favors rendered are remembered and expected to be returned. *Guanxi* extends through all social interactions at every level of society. The ubiquitous *guanxi* and the attendant graft, pork and back handers mean that, just as in other political systems we could mention, those at the top tend to wield ever increasing amounts of wealth and power, and in common with politicians elsewhere have very little interest in sharing it.

Except ...

Consider the life and work of Ted Mack. He happens to have been an Australian, much to that nation's credit. While he was mayor of North Sydney he sold the mayoral Mercedes Benz and used the proceeds to buy buses for public service. When he was a state member of Parliament he deliberately retired two days before he would have become eligible for a comfortable pension. Then he was elected to public office at the federal level. Once again he timed a deliberate retirement, again to render himself ineligible for pension benefits. He opened meetings to the public view, and he made all tenders from private contractors transparent. Shouldn't there be a film about this guy?

Atheistic guanxi is the current orthodoxy in Chinese political structure. My Chinese language teacher in Beijing responded with approval when she asked if I followed any religion, and I told her "No." I lacked the vocabulary to discuss the distinction between spirit and religion. I am not a Buddhist, but I visited a Buddhist temple— one somehow preserved through the Cultural Revolution. When I crossed the threshold I felt the air change. A place of worship holds finer vibrations than a bar that plays poker. I wandered around, admired the huge un-dusted statues of the Buddha, lit some incense, rotated a few prayer wheels, and wondered if official government policy will ever turn again to allow the possibility of worlds beyond the physical.

Once, as a guest teacher in Beijing, I gave a single class examining cartomancy. I introduced the Tarot and Native American animal cards. Mostly the students had no time for such fantastical intuitive tools, and several wrote forthright commentary to that effect. One girl was an exception. She had drawn the card of the Dragonfly, keeper of exquisite and beautiful dreams and illusions. She read and re-read the interpretations given in the book that goes with those cards, followed me to the next class, and with shy, profound courtesy said "I did not know such a thing existed. I cannot thank you enough."

What a privilege to receive such words.

Beijing is a super-megalopolis. In a place of such size there will be contrasts. The functional architecture of the highways, the malls and the forests of high-rise apartment buildings, is the setting where the few architectural survivors of the Cultural Revolution are now listed in guidebooks. The grimy dust prevails everywhere, except in the pristine surfaces at Guo Mao. Travel the number-thirteen subway line and on one side there are seldom-used soccer fields, and on the other a troupe of folk living in a shanty town under a flyover does an early morning martial-arts class.

On one of my flights out of Beijing I left Xi Er Qi with its war-zone dining experience, and I stayed a night at the Beijing Hilton, a brief shuttle ride from the airport. This hotel is built on a scale in line with the dreams of the Emperors. The lobby is a pristine multi-thousand-square-foot area, littered with comfortable sofas and lined with reflective marble paneling. I greeted the lady at the check-in, in Putonghua. Literally, Putonghua means "common tongue". China chose Mandarin with its four tones to be the national language, and now uses a simplified version of it. They also considered Cantonese with its six tones. As I've observed before…those tones! I said that I wanted an early-morning call. At least I think that's what I said. The check-in lady's cheeks went slightly pink. We quickly changed to English. Almost all educated people in China speak it better than I speak Chinese.

I called Dan, who was still in the high-rise apartment with its industrial views.

"I'm back in the first world. Deluxe version."

And the global environment?

Well, take a few situational items at random. If you go to Florida the word is that you are getting a dose of your neighbor's medication every time you drink water from the tap. The ever growing tonnage of plastic waste floats in the northern Pacific, turning the ocean toxic. Fracking continues, whilst energy companies proclaim themselves newly green.

Watch the political processes, East and West—the government backing of corporate interest and the mighty transfer of public funds into private hands. Ask yourself, "This? This! This is what we pay them for?"

It's enough to make you into a revolutionary isn't it?

Political!?

Some of the views expressed here could be seen as subversive. That's why I'm glad I persuaded the Asia-watching journalist China Clompmilly to guest-write this essay.

The fact that the names of the other writers mentioned each contain the same letters as my own is pure coincidence.

Why?

I registered a company. The mission was to produce Western theater in China. I became a producer.

In my patchwork-quilt career I've also been a sometime actor, writer, director and teacher. Producing is the one thing in theater that can't be done without money. Everything else, and I speak from experience on this, can be. Many actors have a day job. Acting is my day job while I'm producing.

I gave presentations for prospective investors. One time a wealthy lady wrote a check and sent it to me. It was for a significant amount of several thousand dollars. I decided to bank it directly. So I went up to 165 West Forty-sixth Street in New York City and took the elevator to the fourteenth floor, where the Actors' Federal Credit Union keeps its offices—and, by the way issues its members with a debit card bearing the oxymoronic legend "ActorCash." When I presented the check, excited that the company account would soon show a credit balance, and that we would be able to put plans into effect, the teller noticed that there was a discrepancy between the words and the figures. She told me that she could only credit me with the smaller amount, the one in figures, and we had a brief argument about it—about four minutes worth.

I took the elevator downstairs and went out into West Forty-sixth Street. Right there, in the middle of the street, a friend whom I had not seen for a few years called my name and we had a few minutes of catch up—maybe another four minutes.

I crossed Times Square and went into the building where I was due to hold another presentation. I wanted to check out the access. I went up the escalator and then down it. No problem, another three minutes. I came out into Times Square and debated with myself whether to turn right to the subway or cross the road and walk along Broadway.

Standing in front of me on one of the areas of the street that had been painted bright blue to indicate a pedestrian area, and maybe six or seven feet diagonally to my left, was an attractive young woman absorbed in a cell phone conversation. She was standing at the edge of the blue area, oblivious to what was happening around her. And that's when the world went into slow motion.

A bus was approaching at some speed. It was maybe thirty feet from the young woman. It honked its horn. Twice. The woman did not hear.

Why?

I stepped forward, grabbed her bicep, and yanked her backward. As she turned in surprise we both saw the edge of the bus pass through the space where she had been standing. I let go of her arm and we looked at each other.

"You saved my life." she said. Her tone was mildly accusatory.

"Yes." I agreed.

"You saved my life." she said again.

We were both stunned. Me, so much so, that even in passionate money-raising mode as I was, I did not say "Hey! Yes I did. Maybe we should go and have coffee, because if you're looking to get into China, I have just the thing for you!" None of that occurred to me.

It was an oddly awkward moment. I half smiled and half winced, amazed at the timetable of destiny that had delivered me with such millimeter-exact precision to that place at that time. Ten seconds—no, three seconds later—and I would have been too late.

Sometimes it's not about the money.

I once met a man who told me he worked for the CIA. "Are you a spy?" I asked him.

"Yes." he said.

"I didn't think spies were allowed to admit that."

"Well," he said, "I'm semi-retired."

We became friendly, and discreet stories from his long diplomatic service were fascinating. We talked about China, and he said something that was a great inspiration to me. He said, "What you're doing is important—the arts are a way for us to say to each other, 'We're not monsters.'"

I believed it to be true. Still believe it actually.

Made in the USA
Charleston, SC
01 April 2013